THE DRIVING BIBLE FOR TEENS

Master Defensive Driving Skills, Overcome Fear & Worry,
and Gain Independence on the Road

JASON ARROTT

TABLE OF CONTENTS

INTRODUCTION

My journey as a driving instructor and advocate for road safety has always been characterized by a fierce desire to empower the young drivers of the next generation. The open road is a symphony of possibilities, a pathway to independence, and an exciting world of its own. However, navigating this world with confidence requires not just a technical understanding of driving but also a mindset that respects and understands the symbiotic relationship we share with other drivers on the road. This conviction forms the basis of this book, *The Driving Bible for Teens.*

Much like a musician who learns to play in harmony with the orchestra, a driver must learn to harmoniously navigate roads shared with others. By striking a balance between assertiveness and courtesy, awareness and decision-making, we can create an environment that's safer and more enjoyable for everyone.

In this book, you'll embark on a journey of mastering defensive driving skills, overcoming the common fears and anxieties associated with driving, and, most importantly, gaining independence on the road. The purpose is to make driving not just an act but a skill, not just a responsibility but a joy.

From understanding the importance of defensive driving, familiarizing yourself with road signs, learning vehicle operations, handling different traffic conditions, and preparing for your DMV written test, we will walk through these steps together. But our exploration doesn't stop there. We delve into the subtler nuances of safe and smart driving, such as managing distractions, handling aggressive drivers, and maintaining mental well-being.

But perhaps most importantly, this book seeks to impart the sense of responsibility that comes with being behind the wheel. Driving is a freedom and a privilege, and with it comes an important duty to keep ourselves and others safe on the road.

Written with compassion and years of experience, this book aims to guide you through your own journey on the road—a journey that I promise will be as exciting as it is transformative. So, buckle up, start your engines, and let's get ready to navigate the highways and byways of the great adventure that is driving.

CHAPTER 1

THE BASICS OF SAFE AND SMART DRIVING

B e safe and smart driving is a year-long public education and awareness campaign aimed at reducing crashes and saving lives. A smart and safe mindset is essential for driving success. Some new drivers believe that mastery of mechanics is all that is required to become a good driver. Successful drivers, in my opinion, are those who have a smart and safe mindset. A smart and safe mindset is essential for driving success. Some new drivers believe that mastery of mechanics is all that is required to become a good driver. Successful drivers, in my opinion, are those who have a smart and safe mindset. My goal is to raise awareness among drivers about their own risky driving habits. The way a driver acts and reacts behind the wheel can mean the difference between a safe trip and a fatal crash.

UNDERSTANDING THE IMPORTANCE OF DEFENSIVE DRIVING

Defensive driving is a collection of driving skills that are necessary in order to keep the driver aware of potential road hazards. Some defensive driving methods are acquired on the road rather than in a driving course. Defensive driving can assist drivers in cautiously reducing any risks involved with on-road driving. Defensive driving techniques are critical for reducing headaches when driving. Commercial industries benefit from defensive driving instruction because it reduces liability connected with dangerous driving.

Being an attentive driver, as well as keeping an eye out for the driver who isn't, is becoming increasingly important. While drivers cannot control the conduct of other drivers, there are many defensive driving abilities that can help drivers reduce the hazards created by other drivers' bad driving habits.

Raises Awareness

The primary goal of defensive driving and safety is to become familiar with all potential hazards and how to avoid them. Awareness is always important in defensive driving since it alerts you to any impending dangers as well as the activities of other road users. Being mindful allows you to perform more effectively while driving. You may avoid incidents that could land you in trouble by driving defensively. Safety and defensive driving allow you to monitor your mirrors for potential risks before becoming caught up in strange scenarios.

Confidence

Defensive driving instruction teaches drivers to avoid becoming overconfident behind the wheel. We all think we're great drivers until we make stupid mistakes that could have been avoided with a little more confidence on the road. In most cases, it is our overconfidence conviction that gets us into problems. Even if you are certain of something, you may rush at a fast speed, which will lead to issues. You must, however, regulate your confidence on the road with defensive driving. While driving, you must have trust, yet overconfidence might lead to serious traffic violations.

Making Informed Decisions

Defensive driving is one of the most important road safety strategies. You may not be able to control the actions of other drivers, but defensive driving allows you to make quick judgments that will help to protect your life and property, as well as the lives and properties of other reckless road users. Defensive driving puts you in a solid position where you can make informed decisions since you are aware of the ramifications of other road users' unsafe conduct.

Slow Driving

You will be more cautious on the road if you are well-versed in road safety and defensive driving. It allows you to drive more slowly than the surrounding traffic. This is especially important when driving in bad weather.

Create an Escape Strategy

You have an advantage over those who don't know anything about it if you have these skills. This learning may take up your time, but it is all worthwhile. You can be a good driver, but you won't be safe on the road until you prepare an escape route while you're on the road. Defensive driving allows you to devise a speedy escape plan, which is vital. Instead of swerving off the road, defensive drivers change lanes.

DEVELOPING A RESPONSIBLE AND ALERT MINDSET

Developing a responsible and vigilant mindset is essential for defensive driving practice. It refers to a set of skills and behaviors that enable drivers to anticipate and respond to potential road hazards. Drivers who adopt this mindset actively priorities safety, not only for themselves but also for other road users. Every aspect of defensive driving, from maintaining a safe following distance to remaining attentive and focused, contributes to the development of a responsible and alert mindset.

Safe and Steady Driving

The basis of defensive driving is safe and steady driving. It is best to drive at the speed limit while keeping up with the traffic flow. Avoid abrupt stops, quick speed changes, and unexpected lane changes. To ensure adequate reaction time, keep a safe following distance of one car length for every 10 mph of travel speed.

Preparation for a Safe Journey

Preparation is critical to ensuring a safe voyage. Wearing seat belts is mandatory for all vehicle occupants. If you need directions, it is also a good idea to program an audio navigation system ahead of time. Checking traffic and road conditions provides for better planning, allowing drivers to avoid routes that are congested, work zones, school zones, or other potential hazards.

Enhancing Visibility and Observation Skills

Visibility and keen observation are essential to ensure safe driving. Utilizing turn signals effectively communicates your intentions to other road users, while headlights are crucial for illuminating the way in low-light conditions. Regular maintenance of brakes and taillights promotes their optimal functionality. Always make sure that windows, mirrors, and glasses are clean to avoid any visual obstructions. A regular check of the rearview and side mirrors helps maintain a clear view of your surroundings. Make a habit of scanning the road for potential hazards and being aware of other vehicles' actions. Pay particular attention to large trucks and be conscious of blind spots to keep safe distances.

Concentration and Attention

Defensive driving demands unwavering concentration and attention. Steering clear of distractions such as eating, reading, grooming, reaching for objects, using electronic devices, or engaging in intense conversations is vital to maintain your focus on the road. It's equally important to refrain from driving when impaired due to alcohol, drugs, medication, fatigue, or physical discomfort. Your safety hinges on fully committing your attention to driving.

Anticipation and Response

Effective anticipation of potential hazards can be lifesaving on the road. Drivers must always be prepared to predict the movements of other motorists, bicyclists, motorcyclists, commercial vehicles, and pedestrians. Defensive driving mandates quick, effective responses to unexpected situations, whether on side streets, driveways, parking lots, or when other vehicles switch lanes. Be especially cautious in work zones, crossroads, and school zones. Respect and follow the directions of traffic signs and flaggers to ensure a smooth flow of traffic.

Intersection Safety and Adapting to Weather Conditions

Intersections can be tricky, and defensive driving skills are vital in navigating them safely. Be sure to check for cross traffic from all directions before proceeding, and never assume that other drivers will automatically yield. Adherence to posted speed limits and remaining distraction-free, particularly in school zones, is a must. When weather conditions are poor, remember to slow down and increase the distance between vehicles. By doing so, you'll help create a safer driving environment for everyone on the road.

FAMILIARIZING YOURSELF WITH ROAD SIGNS AND THEIR MEANINGS

Traffic signs are quite significant in terms of road safety. You are bound to see one of these signs as soon as you peek out the window onto the streets. Safety signs have been around for a long time, offering regulations, caution, and direction information to everyone traveling on roads, whether they are vehicles or pedestrians. These are placed on roadways to ensure that all drivers are aware of traffic rules and to warn motorists of potential hazards. Accidents are more likely to occur in the absence of these.

Signs for traffic and parking should be an integral part of your facility's safety and identification program. There are numerous varieties of traffic and parking signs, each with its own purpose. Therefore it is critical that you understand which sign will best suit your individual needs. Posting the incorrect sign in a critical area, or failing to display a sign at all, might make the difference between smooth traffic flow and a chaotic disaster. It can also be the difference between life and death in some circumstances. One important road sign category you should be familiar with is regulatory signs and their purpose on your land.

Regulatory Signs: Establishing Rules and Ensuring Safety on the Road

Regulatory signs are generally used to establish road rules, but they are also used to help control traffic flow and movement. These, sometimes known as required signs, must always be observed by drivers. If drivers do not comply, legal action may be taken against the driver or, in rare situations, against you directly.

Right-of-Way Symbols

These traffic signs are commonly seen at junctions as the STOP or YIELD sign. Posting these signs in key sections of your facility's parking lot, loading area, and even private roadways aids in establishing the right-of-way for work vehicles, employees, and visitors.

Signs that say, "Do Not Enter."

A do not enter sign is sometimes all that stands between a driver and a potentially disastrous mistake, such as entering a one-way lane. Do not enter signs can help you restrict traffic in parking lots, loading areas, and even warehouses.

Signs Denoting Speed Limits

These signs, as the name implies, are used to enforce a maximum speed that has been determined to be safe for that specific region. These signs serve a crucial part in the safety of workers, visitors, and the like, whether they are on a commercial highway, within a warehouse monitoring forklift traffic, or in your facility's parking lot.

Parking Symbols

Display these signs to show where parking is authorized, the type of vehicle permitted, and the duration of parking. These are also used to display parking limits or prohibitions in a parking space or building.

Pedestrian Zone Markers

These sign styles, like some of the other traffic signs described, can be used both inside and outside the institution to help ensure the safety of individuals walking on foot. It is beneficial to provide safe walking spaces to avoid colliding with a moving vehicle, whether it is a car, a truck, or a forklift.

CHAPTER 2

MASTERING THE FUNDAMENTALS OF DRIVING

Driving is a necessary ability that allows people to have freedom, convenience, and independence. It does, however, come with a lot of responsibility. Mastering the foundations of driving is critical for guaranteeing one's own and others' safety on the road. Drivers can negotiate varied traffic circumstances with confidence and lower the chances of accidents by having a solid foundation of driving skills and knowledge.

PREPARING FOR YOUR FIRST DRIVE

Driving gives you a lot of freedom, but it also comes with a lot of responsibility, which many new learner drivers aren't used to. The prospect of driving a car may seem intimidating at first, and you may be apprehensive. The right driving instructor, on the other hand, will put you in the right mindset, giving you the confidence to stay cool behind the wheel and allowing you to think clearly in situations that could be difficult without your certified experience.

It's a good idea to receive some driving tips before your first session to ensure you're prepared. This chapter will provide you with nine recommendations for your first driving lesson to help you relax. What you can expect from your first driving lesson. Here are some pointers for your initial driving lesson:

Get Plenty of Sleep

Getting 7-9 hours of sleep before your first driving lesson will keep you energized, aware, and ready for any obstacles that may come. According to research, getting adequate sleep is essential for "procedural memory" - the type of memory that helps you learn how to learn tasks like driving a car. To get a decent night's sleep before your first driving lesson, avoid caffeine and devices before bed.

Get Familiar with A Car's Layout

While some cars have distinct layouts, such as a handbrake lever on the right rather than the left, they are essentially the same.

If you know the car you're driving, become acquainted with the following:

- Pedal for acceleration
- The brake pedals.
- The steering wheel
- Lights and indicators
- Mirrors in the rearview
- Clutch pedal (only in manuals)
- The gear sticks.
- The instrument panel on the dashboard

Ensure You're Hydrated and Nourished Ahead of Your Lesson

One of the most important pieces of advice for your first driving lesson is to drink enough water and eat healthily. You'll be able to perform and concentrate much better, and you don't want to be hungry when learning to drive. I also recommend that you bring a water bottle to the lesson and keep it in a safe and easily accessible location.

Wear Appropriate Shoes and Clothing

Wear comfortable shoes that allow you to move freely from the brake to the accelerator. Wear comfortable clothing that allows you to freely move your arms and legs and turn your body to glance over your shoulder when reversing and changing lanes.

Listen to What Your Instructor Is Saying

It may seem foolish, but the exhilaration and anticipation of driving for the first time can make it difficult to concentrate. So, pay close attention to what your driving teacher says to ensure you become a more confident driver at the end of the class.

Stay Focused

Keep an eye on the dashboard lights and indicators, pay attention to the road ahead, and keep an eye out for potential hazards all around you. Pay attention to your instructor when he or she is speaking to you. Focus on listening to your instructor and doing what they suggest or ask throughout your first driving session. However, you will not have to cope with everything all at once; your instructor will take it one step at a time.

You'll grow used to juggling all these things over time, and once you've learned how to prioritize your attention with a little help from your driving instructor, you might discover it's easier than you imagined, which brings us to tip number eight.

Relax

Remember that your first driving lesson is not a driving exam, and your instructor will not ask you to accomplish anything sophisticated.

Depending on the driving teacher, you will most likely be learning the fundamentals of the vehicle and may not even be allowed to drive in traffic.

Many driving instructors will treat your first lesson as your introduction to driving and will structure a lesson that helps you familiarize yourself with the inside of their car (especially if you don't already know where everything is located) before eventually getting you to drive around in a parking lot or quiet backstreet away from traffic. If you make a mistake, listen to your instructor, try and apply what they tell you, and learn from the experience.

LEARNING VEHICLE CONTROLS AND OPERATIONS

When beginning the route to becoming a proficient driver, it is critical to become acquainted with the various car controls and procedures. Mastering the controls and operations of a vehicle can often feel like learning a new language. From turn signal indicators to the nuances of the accelerator pedal, understanding these elements is integral to becoming a proficient driver. So buckle up, and let's embark on this in-depth exploration of vehicle controls and operations.

The Steering Wheel

The steering wheel is not just a wheel; it's your primary tool for guiding your vehicle on the road. It might look plain, but the modern steering wheel hosts a variety of controls. From activating the car's horn to managing cruise control, audio settings, or Bluetooth hands-free phone systems, these controls help you operate various features without taking your hands off the wheel. But remember, the primary function of the steering wheel is to control the vehicle's direction - an important task that demands your undivided attention.

The Accelerator and Brake

Nestled at your feet are two critical controls: the accelerator and the brake pedals. The accelerator, situated to the right, controls the engine's speed, thus governing your vehicle's velocity. Pressing down on the accelerator feeds more fuel to the engine, increasing its speed and, consequently, the speed of your vehicle.

On the left of the accelerator lies the brake pedal, the function of which is pretty self-explanatory: it slows down your vehicle or brings it to a halt. Braking needs to be done gradually to avoid abrupt stops that could potentially lead to collisions.

The Gear Shift

The gear shift, often located between the driver and front passenger seat, manages your vehicle's transmission. Depending on your vehicle, you may have a manual or automatic transmission.

For manual transmission vehicles, the gear shift allows you to manually select the appropriate gear for your speed, including a reverse gear for backing up. Accompanying the gear shift is a third pedal—the clutch—used to disengage the gears while shifting.

In automatic vehicles, the gear shift lever typically has settings for Park (P), Reverse (R), Neutral (N), Drive (D), and sometimes a lower gear (L). Understandably, knowing when and how to use these settings is fundamental for smooth and safe driving.

Turn Indicators and Headlights

Turn signal indicators, often located on a lever to the left of the steering wheel, help communicate your driving intentions to others on the road. Signaling before turning or changing lanes keeps both you and other drivers safe.

Similarly, the control for headlights is crucial for visibility. Located typically on the dashboard or a lever on the steering column, it lets you switch between various modes like daytime running lights, low beams, and high beams and often includes the control for fog lights. Correct usage of these lights is vital for your visibility to other drivers, especially in low-light conditions or inclement weather.

Tracking Speed and Distance

The speedometer and odometer are two essential gauges displayed on your vehicle's dashboard. The speedometer tells you how fast you're moving, which is vital to comply with speed limits and ensure safe driving conditions.

The odometer, on the other hand, logs the total distance that your vehicle has traveled since its production. This tool is essential for maintenance schedules and determining your vehicle's overall usage and potential resale value.

The Emergency Controller: Parking Brake

Often relegated to the side, the parking brake, also known as the emergency or handbrake, is another crucial control. Generally found to the right of the driver's seat or as a pedal on the far left, the parking brake assists in securing the vehicle when parked, particularly on inclines, and serves as a backup braking system in case of brake failure.

PRACTICING ESSENTIAL DRIVING MANEUVERS

Now it's time to talk about the fundamental driving skills you'll need to handle your vehicle safely and avoid collisions with other drivers. Most of your learning will be done behind the wheel for practical driving actions like steering, backing up, and signaling; there is no alternative for getting out there and putting these abilities into practice.

Before you begin, consider the following:

When you take your driving test, the examiner will expect you to complete a thorough pre-drive checklist. The first item in this module will walk you through the process, but you should also consult the official DMV pre-drive checklist to ensure you are following the steps correctly. A pre-drive checklist serves three primary purposes:

a. Check for any obstacles around the vehicle (including people and animals) that could make pulling out of your parking spot dangerous.
b. To ensure that the car is safe to drive. Check for flat tires, fluid leaks, and dirt on the windows or mirrors that may affect your vision of the road.

To make any necessary vehicle adjustments. Changing the height of the driver's seat or the angle of the rearview mirror, for example.

Once the pre-drive checklist is completed, you should double-check the placement of a few critical components that were not included in the list. You will almost certainly be working with an unfamiliar car while taking your driving test. As a result, before you leave, locate the controls for the lights, windshield wipers, horn, and other important components so you don't have to look for them while driving.

Positioning the Vehicle

All public roads are divided into lanes. Traffic lanes are marked out using broken or solid pavement markings, except for particularly rural routes; you will learn more about what these painted lines imply in a later module of this course. One of the first things you must learn as a learner driver is how to place oneself within a lane. It is not simply a matter of situating your vehicle in the center of a lane. However, this is where you will spend most of your time. There are five separate lane positions to learn, and you will occupy each of them for different reasons.

    a. Lane position 1: In the center of the lane.

    b. Lane position 2: Aligned to the lane's left.

    c. Lane 3: Aligned to the right side of the lane.

    d. Lane 4: straddles the left dividing line.

    e. Lane 5: straddling the right dividing line.

The first lane is your default position. If there are no forthcoming changes in the roadway that require you to alter your position to preserve safety, this is the position you will take. Lane positions two through five will be assumed only when avoiding close dangers or preparing to turn.

The simple part is learning the various lane placements. When you first start driving, it can be difficult to maneuver the vehicle into these positions because the vehicle itself will impede your view of the road. Fortunately, we can find the correct alignment by using reference points around the vehicle.

Using Vehicle Reference Points

It will take time to learn how to properly position your car, whether changing lanes, parking, or stopping at a traffic signal. Because the vehicle's hood, trunk, and doors obscure your view of the road, you'll need a separate set of visual car reference points to figure out where you are in relation to other objects and marks. These reference points are built inside the vehicle.

Because each car model has its own distinct size and shape, reference points may differ slightly from vehicle to vehicle. This module's information will assist you in locating usable reference points on your vehicle. The concept of car reference points is straightforward: from the driver's seat, you cannot see the road surface immediately around the vehicle, but you can see some external features of the car (such as the hood and headlights) and parts of the road slightly further away from the car (such as the curb and lane markings). As a result, you can align sections of the car with what you observe on the road to assume a precise position.

The main reference points we will discuss in this section are:

- When parking on the left side of the road, preparing to turn left, assuming lane position two, or aligning oneself with any left-side neighboring object, you will use this reference point.

- The hood's center: this will assist you in parking on the right side of the road, preparing for a right turn, assuming lane position three, or aligning yourself with any right-side neighboring item.

- The side mirrors will assist you in effectively positioning yourself in relation to "STOP" lines and other front barriers.

The door handles will assist you in accurately positioning the vehicle when looking over your shoulder to reverse the car. Reference points will also assist you in securely sharing the road with vulnerable road users. You can ensure that nearby cyclists and motorcyclists have appropriate room if you know exactly where your car is in a lane.

Steering Techniques

car reference points can assist you in accurately positioning your car in preparation for upcoming turns. Your grasp of steering tactics will determine how safely and effectively you can execute those maneuvers. Assuming the proper hand position is the first step in learning how to use the steering wheel. We'll go through the three most often used steering wheel hand positions, as well as the benefits and drawbacks of each. They are as follows:

- The 10 and 2 position - this is the standard steering wheel hand position that provides adequate leverage and comfort.

- The 9 and 3 position is slightly less comfortable than the "10 and 2" position, but it is safer since it keeps the driver's forearms away from the airbag deployment zone.

- The 8 and 4 position is more comfortable and safer than the "9 and 3" posture. However, it does not provide the same level of leverage.

Let's get back to working on those turns. There are correct strategies for turning the steering wheel to the left or right, just as there are suitable hand positions for the steering wheel. Under certain conditions, all the steering approaches discussed in this section are suitable. They are as follows:

- Hand-to-hand steering entails feeding the steering wheel with your hands.
- Hand-over-hand steering, in which your hands are crossed.
- One-handed steering, in which only one hand remains on the steering wheel as it turns.

You should not be penalized for employing any of these strategies during your practical driving test if you do so correctly. You will not fail for steering with one hand on the steering wheel while backing up the vehicle, but you will most likely fail if you do it while driving forwards and executing a turn. Steering with one hand is unnecessary in this case and would reduce your control over the car.

Backing Up and Reversing

Reversing the vehicle is always more difficult and riskier than driving forward since your view of the road behind the automobile is severely limited. You'll need to turn your upper body in the driver's seat while still working the controls in front of you to see where you're heading. In real-world driving conditions, unless it is the safest alternative, you should avoid driving in reverse. When it comes to preparing for your driving test, we recommend practicing backing up the vehicle as much as possible. This critical skill will be evaluated during the exam.

Start learning to drive in reverse only after you've mastered controlling your speed and steering while going forward. When the time comes, the step-by-step backup guide in this book will be of assistance. Keep in mind that your side-view and rear-view mirrors will be useful when backing up, but you should not rely only on them. If you do a reverse maneuver in your driving test without turning to look over your shoulder, the examiner will most certainly fail you.

Acceleration Techniques

To accelerate, put pressure on the accelerator pedal to inject more fuel into the engine. It is critical to gradually increase pressure on this pedal in order to maintain control and avoid "jerky" acceleration. You should use the ball of your foot while keeping your heel firmly planted on the automobile floor. This will allow you to easily swap between the accelerator and brake pedals if you need to slow down.

Different road conditions necessitate different acceleration tactics. Maintaining speed while driving uphill, for example, will necessitate a progressive increase in gas pedal pressure, even if you are not attempting to move any faster. Hazardous driving conditions, as well as entering a highway, will necessitate distinct acceleration skills, which are discussed in this subsection.

Slowing Down and Stopping

Applying pressure to the service brake pedal causes the car to slow down. As with acceleration, there is a lot more to safe and successful braking than merely pressing the pedal to the floor and praying for the best. Even in an emergency, pressing your foot down on the brake pedal is rarely the best option. The sort of braking system used by your car will determine how you must use your brakes. Most current automobiles have an antilock braking system (ABS) that regulates braking force on the driver's behalf. If your car lacks ABS, you must learn threshold braking tactics to keep the wheels from losing traction. All new drivers must become acquainted with this skill to some level, as they may one day be obliged to drive a non-ABS vehicle or an ABS vehicle whose system has failed.

It is critical to master effective braking tactics. You may be unable to stop in a dangerous scenario if you use your brakes ineffectively, and you will likely cause early wear to your vehicle's braking system.

Signaling your Intentions

To properly communicate with other drivers on the road, you must learn to use your turn indicators, headlights, taillights, and car horns. Learning hand signals is also a crucial part of your driver's education program, which we will go over lower down on this page.

Your turn indicator lights will be your primary signaling tool. Their primary role is to alert other drivers that you intend to turn or change lanes, but they can also be utilized in an emergency to replace your warning lights. Turn signals should be engaged at least 100 feet before a turn and should remain on until the move is completed. When your turn signals fail, use hand signals instead.

When you apply the brakes, your taillights will illuminate, signaling to other drivers that your car is slowing. When you need to slow down, you can modify your taillights if a car is tailgating or following too closely. In this case, get their attention by softly pulsating the brake pedal and flashing the taillights several times.

Headlight Flashing

To attract the attention of other cars, headlights might be flashed. The only legal reason to flash your headlights at another driver, according to most state driving manuals, is to tell them that their high-beam headlights are on. If a driver approaches you with their high beams on, you can alert them to the situation by flashing your own headlights at them many times. If they do not decrease their lights, avert your gaze to the right side of the road to avoid being blinded, and do not retaliate by using your own high beams.

If other cars' headlights flash at you, check your own high-beam indicator, as this is most likely the cause. If your high beams aren't the problem, it could be that they're alerting you to a misaligned or defective headlight. Check them out with a mechanic as soon as possible.

Flashing headlights to alert other vehicles of a speed trap or police presence on the road is a prevalent practice throughout the United States. We strongly advise you to consult your state's driving manual for more information on this subject. It is unlawful in some states.

Hand Signals

If your turn indicators or taillights fail, you must use hand signals to express your desire to turn, slow down, or stop. They'll also come in handy on bright days when your signal lights are hard to see and your indicators are obscured by a line of traffic. You will not be spotted if you utilize hand signals at night. You simply cannot drive after dark if your signal lights are not operational.

All signals must be sent via the left window, as indicated here:

- A right turn is made by extending your left arm and bending it at the elbow, with your hand pointing upward.
- A left turn is performed by extending your left arm straight out with no bend. Your left hand should be pointing.

- When slowing or stopping, extend your left arm and bend it at the elbow, with your hand pointed down towards the road.

Don't ignore hand signals during your driver's education program; you'll need them more than you think! Most drivers are fortunate enough not to require hand signals, but they must identify them. Cyclists do not have signal lights and must communicate via hand signals.

Using Your Car Horn

Your car horn is a very powerful communication instrument that you should use sparingly. Many drivers are far too ready to honk their horns in annoyance, anger, or merely to greet other drivers. The car horn was not designed to be used for self-expression but rather as a last resort when you absolutely need to draw another driver's attention.

When you blow your horn, you risk frightening other drivers and risking an accident. Use your automobile horn only when essential to protect yourself or other road users. As an example:

- When you need to warn another driver that they're about to hit you.
- When you have lost control of your vehicle, and must alert oncoming traffic.
- When it is necessary to scare an animal off the road in order to avoid an accident.
- In low visibility conditions and when approaching blind curves, certain states allow for the mild use of the car horn.

Never use your horn to show frustration, encourage other drivers to move or travel quicker (unless necessary to avoid a collision), or greet another car. You should also avoid blowing your horn when there are horses or horse-drawn vehicles on the road unless absolutely required.

Using Driving Lanes

One of the most crucial abilities you will develop as a student driver is the ability to anticipate and prepare for forthcoming lane changes. Knowing which lane to take on a two-lane road with traffic moving in both directions is simple. On multi-lane roads with traffic lights, interchanges, or various streams of traffic traveling in the same direction, things become a little more complicated. Fortunately, the principles for selecting the correct lane in such situations are among the most basic you will study throughout your education. Our "Using Driving Lanes" module will guide you through the process.

When choosing a lane on a multi-lane highway, the most important guideline to remember is to keep right. The right lane is intended for the slowest traffic on the route and is usually the lane you must use if you wish to exit at an approaching intersection. If you need to pass another driver or create room for new traffic on the road, merge left into an adjacent lane.

You must learn to carefully arrange your lane shifts, avoiding all except the most critical instances. Merging into a new lane always raises the level of risk you are exposed to when driving since it disrupts the situation on the roadway surrounding your car. In this part, we break down the ideal method for changing lanes into simple steps. Changing lanes without following this technique is risky and could result in you failing your driving test or receiving a traffic citation if you are already certified.

Merging is the process of joining a new lane of traffic (typically when approaching or quitting a roadway). Mergers, like changing lanes, must be carried out in compliance with safety rules. When you are a new driver, seek a four-second gap between vehicles to accommodate your vehicle. There may be occasions when you need to enter a narrower space, but for the time being, this is the rule you must follow.

Entering and Exiting Highways

Merging onto high-speed, limited-access motorways is difficult and should be undertaken only by experienced beginner drivers. To merge safely, use the acceleration lane to increase your speed to match that of the existing traffic on the route. Exiting the freeway is perhaps easier, provided you plan of time. Never cross multiple lanes of traffic at the same time or merge into the deceleration lane in a hurry. It is preferable to miss your exit than to collide.

Turning Maneuvers

Making turns safely and successfully necessitates strong steering control abilities, comprehension of diverse lane uses, and knowledge of the road rules applicable to that stretch of road. In "Making Turns", we go through the two basic sorts of turns you'll need to make when driving:

- Turning at junctions (which may include turning left, right, protected or unprotected turns, using a center-left turn lane, and observing traffic signals)
- Making a U-turn, two-point turn, or three-point turn to point your vehicle in the opposite direction (reversing your course of travel)

With the material covered in this section of the course, you will be able to successfully and securely perform all fundamental turning maneuvers. When it comes to crossroads, you should never assume the turn is safe to make. Even if a traffic control device indicates that you have the right-of-way, you should always properly examine the roadway for opposing streams of traffic. Every day, drivers make stupid mistakes at crossings. If this occurs, your alertness and caution may be the only thing separating you from a collision.

Passing other Vehicles

Passing another car may need briefly enter an opposite traffic lane. Even on generally clean roads, this technique has a lot of potential pitfalls. Passing another car solely to "get ahead" is a risk that should be avoided. However, because passing is the safest course of action in some cases, you must know how to perform a pass safely and legally.

In addition to reviewing the information in this module, consult your driver's manual for the laws that govern when you can and cannot pass another vehicle in your state. In general, passing is prohibited if:

- For at least 800 feet, you cannot see the road ahead.
- You are driving through an intersection or within 100 feet of an intersection (other jurisdictions have differing laws on this).
- You're only 100 feet away from a tunnel, bridge, or railway crossing.
- You're stuck behind a stalled school bus.

Passing is prohibited on this stretch of road, according to traffic control devices.

If you have determined that it is allowed to perform a pass on a stretch of road, you must then consider if it is safe and worth it. When you're satisfied you want to go ahead with the maneuver, the step-by-step passing guide in this course will walk you through it. Before attempting a pass in a real-world driving situation, make sure you are comfortable with this knowledge!

Parking Maneuvers

Learning when, where, and how to park are important skills that many new drivers miss. Every state highway code distinguishes between parking and momentarily halting to load or unload a vehicle. To prevent infringing the law, you should consult your state handbook for local information on this subject. Stopping temporarily is legal in many situations; however, parking the car is not. The information we provide covers parking rules and restrictions as they apply in most places, while your city or state may have some small changes.

You must learn multiple parking procedures in order to properly park your vehicle in various scenarios. They are as follows:

- Perpendicular parking occurs when the vehicle is parked at a 90-degree angle to flowing traffic.
- Angle parking occurs when a vehicle is parked at a 45-degree angle to move traffic.
- Parallel parking means parking parallel to moving traffic. These areas are typically located near city streets.
- Parking on a hill means that the vehicle is parked on a slope that points upwards or downhill.

This necessitates additional safety precautions. Even experienced drivers often find parking to be a difficult experience. To reduce the stress of attempting to find a parking space at the last minute, consider choosing a "less convenient" location that is further from your destination.

Mastering Driving Maneuvers

You should not expect to read through this lesson once and have all the information you need to be committed to memory - there is a lot to take in! You should review this knowledge as often as possible until you have mastered these important driving tactics.

Remember that a session or two with a certified instructor is essential if you want to pass the driving test the first time. Driving instructors are educated to get you through the evaluation as well as help you build safe driving habits. With a little coaching from a licensed instructor, you will have a far greater chance of passing and will profit much more from the rest of your driving practice. If you're ready to start learning, let's start with that pre-drive checklist.

NAVIGATING DIFFERENT TRAFFIC CONDITIONS

As drivers, we frequently encounter heavy traffic, freeway driving, construction zones, inclement weather, school zones, and other unusual road conditions. To ensure safety, efficiency, and responsible driving in each of these scenarios, a different approach is required. We can navigate diverse traffic conditions with confidence and contribute to safer roads for everyone by understanding the specific demands of each situation and employing the appropriate techniques.

Maintaining a Safe Following Distance

It is critical to maintain an adequate following distance from the vehicle in front when driving in heavy traffic. This creates a buffer zone and allows for faster reaction time in the event of a sudden stop or an emergency. Drivers can avoid rear-end collisions and lessen the impact of sudden changes in traffic flow by maintaining a safe distance.

Using Mirrors Frequently

In heavy traffic, it is critical to constantly monitor the rearview and side mirrors. This allows you to be aware of surrounding vehicles, anticipate lane changes, and make informed decisions based on traffic flow. Regular mirror checks help to identify potential blind spots and provide a complete view of the traffic situation, lowering the risk of an accident.

Signaling Early and Clearly

It is critical to communicate with other drivers and ensure smooth lane changes or turns by signaling intentions early and using indicators clearly. Clear communication reduces confusion and improves traffic flow overall. By signaling ahead of time, drivers give others enough time to react and adjust their driving accordingly, fostering a safer and more predictable road environment.

Avoiding Aggressive Maneuvers

In heavy traffic, it is critical to avoid aggressive maneuvers such as sudden lane changes, tailgating, or excessive speeding. Patience and a calm demeanor help to make driving safer and more enjoyable. Aggressive driving raises tensions and increases the likelihood of a collision. It is critical to maintain composure, exercise restraint, and prioritize safety over impatience.

Staying Calm and Focused

Maintaining a calm and focused mindset in heavy traffic is essential. Avoid distractions, keep tension under control, and be patient. Drivers who maintain their focus are better able to anticipate potential hazards, respond quickly to changing conditions, and make sound decisions. A calm demeanor fosters a positive driving experience and decreases the chances of making mistakes or acting rashly on the road.

Smooth Merging

When entering a freeway, merging smoothly with the flow of traffic is crucial. Before merging, use entrance ramps to accelerate and match the speed of vehicles on the motorway. Yield to approaching traffic and look for a safe gap to merge. Smooth merging aids in the maintenance of a steady traffic flow and reduces disturbances that might lead to congestion or accidents.

Using the Left Lane for Passing

On a motorway, the left lane is usually designated for passing. Use it to overtake slower vehicles when necessary. To preserve a smooth traffic flow, return to the right lane after completing the pass. It is critical to be aware of other drivers and to avoid lingering in the left lane, which can obstruct the progress of faster-moving traffic.

Maintaining a Consistent Speed

Consistency in speed is important on freeways. Maintain a speed that is consistent with traffic flow, allowing for a safe and predictable driving experience. Sudden changes in speed can cause traffic congestion and increase the risk of rear-end collisions. Adapting to traffic speeds helps to keep the freeway's overall rhythm and promotes safer driving conditions.

Checking Blind Spots

Always check blind spots before changing lanes on a motorway to verify there are no vehicles in the next lanes. To ensure a safe lane change, use mirrors and a quick shoulder check. Blind spot monitoring systems can also help detect vehicles that are not visible in mirrors alone. Checking blind spots thoroughly reduces the probability of side-swipe incidents and improves overall lane-change safety.

Paying Attention to Exit Signs and Lanes

Keep an eye out for upcoming exit signs and freeway lanes. Lane shifts should be planned in time to facilitate a smooth transition to the intended exit ramp. Proactive lane positioning and anticipating exit maneuvers reduce last-minute lane changes and the possibility of abrupt braking or lane weaving, which can disrupt traffic flow and endanger other drivers.

Observing lower Speed Limits

Construction zones frequently have lower speed limits for the safety of workers and cars. Maintain a safe environment by adhering to these speed limits. Slowing down gives you more time to react to changing conditions, potential obstacles, and construction equipment, lowering the risk of accidents and ensuring everyone's safety in the work zone.

Lane Markings and Following Signage

In construction zones, pay particular attention to signage and lane markers. They are useful for indicating lane closures, detours, or temporary changes in traffic patterns. Following these instructions helps to keep traffic flowing smoothly and avoids confusion or last-minute maneuvers that could endanger workers or fellow drivers.

Watching for Construction Workers

Keep an eye out for construction workers and their activities in construction zones. Use caution, slow down, and give them enough space to complete their tasks safely. Construction workers are frequently exposed to moving traffic, and their safety is dependent on drivers being alert and considerate. Keep an eye out for flagger signals, follow their instructions, and be patient, as delays may occur due to ongoing construction activities.

Patience

Construction zones can be inconvenient due to traffic delays and lane closures. To ensure the safety of all road users, it is critical to remain patient and follow instructions. Avoid abrupt lane changes, resist the urge to speed through the construction zone, and be courteous to construction workers and other drivers. Patience and collaboration help to ensure a safer and more efficient flow of traffic through construction zones.

Reducing Speed

When driving in inclement weather, such as rain, snow, or fog, reduce your speed to account for decreased visibility and traction on the road. Slowing down improves vehicle control, reduces the risk of skidding or hydroplaning, and gives you more time to react to unexpected hazards or changes in road conditions.

Increasing Following Distance

Maintain a longer following distance in bad weather to allow for longer stopping distances. This provides a safety margin and lowers the likelihood of a collision. Slippery road surfaces necessitate longer braking distances, and the additional space between vehicles provides more time to react and adjust to sudden changes in traffic flow.

Using Headlights and Fog Lights

In low visibility situations, turn on your headlights to improve your visibility to other drivers. If fog lights are available, use them in foggy conditions because they are specifically designed for such situations. Increased visibility lets other drivers see your car more clearly, lowering the likelihood of an accident. During inclement weather, properly functioning lights are critical for making your presence on the road visible to others.

Checking Weather Predictions

It is essential to check weather forecasts before embarking on travel to anticipate any unpleasant conditions along your path. You can plan your trip carefully if you are aware of impending storms, severe rain, or icy conditions. If severe weather is forecast, consider delaying your travel or using other routes to avoid dangerous areas. Being proactive in monitoring weather updates increases your safety and allows you to make better decisions on the road.

Keeping an Eye Out for Pedestrians

Keep an eye out for pedestrians, especially youngsters, in school zones. Expect children to not always obey traffic laws or use marked crosswalks correctly. Slow down and be prepared to come to a complete stop if necessary. Passing school buses should be done with caution, and they should always come to a complete stop when their stop signs are extended. In school zones, being aware and attentive can help to prevent accidents and save the lives of young pedestrians.

Obey Crossing Guard Instructions

School zones frequently have crossing guards who assist pedestrians in crossing the road safely. Respect their commands and signals. When you see a crossing guard, come to a complete stop and wait for them to signal that it is safe to pass. Their presence assures the safe and orderly crossing of youngsters and merits the drivers' full cooperation.

Wildlife Awareness

Meeting wildlife on or near the road is one of the unique problems of rural driving. Animals such as deer, elk, or livestock might dart onto the road unexpectedly, posing a substantial risk to vehicles. Maintain vigilance and keep an eye out for any signs of wildlife presence. Slow down if you see an animal near the road, and be prepared to brake or take evasive action if necessary. Avoid swerving suddenly to avoid hitting an animal, as this can result in loss of control and a collision with another vehicle.

CHAPTER 3
DEFENSIVE DRIVING TECHNIQUES

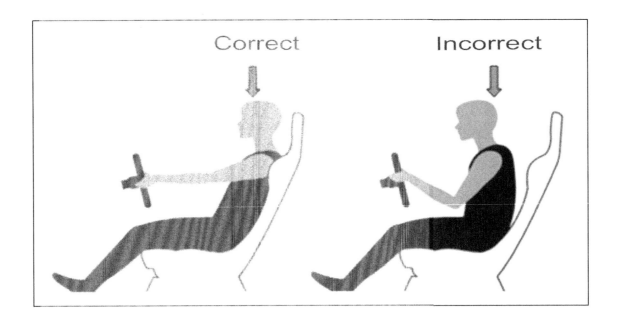

Human mistakes are responsible for almost 95% of road traffic accidents, according to international studies! We can dramatically reduce that percentage by becoming a better and more defensive driver. This chapter will delve into the critical features of defensive driving and analyze the important tactics that can dramatically minimize the danger of road accidents. Defensive driving goes beyond simply knowing the rules of the road and fundamental driving mechanics. It entails having a proactive mindset, being constantly attentive, and being able to foresee and react to impending threats. By using these defensive driving practices, you may improve your road safety and contribute to a better driving environment for everyone.

RECOGNIZING AND AVOIDING COMMON ROAD HAZARDS

When you're driving along the road, unexpected things may appear in front of your vehicle. These unexpected elements can push you to crash into another vehicle and cause an accident if you are not cautious. While it is not always possible to avoid things in your driving lane, it is important to be aware of frequent road dangers and notice them when they meet your car.

From deer to raccoons, animals travel across highways and other roads in search of food or new habitats. Most highways have warning signs for animal crossings to assist you in identifying the most typical animal crossing places, although animals can cross anywhere.

So, do you swerve, or do you not swerve? Experts advise that if you come across an animal and must choose between swerving and not swerving, choose the latter. While you don't want to hit an animal, the repercussions of swerving and maybe colliding with another vehicle are significantly more serious.

Only if there is a moose in the road should you swerve to avoid it. Moose can weigh up to 1,600 pounds and will cause substantial damage to your vehicle if hit. Swerve to avoid creatures other than moose.

Debris on the Road

Road debris occurs in a variety of shapes and sizes. Common road debris includes items from autos, semi-truck spills, and tree branches. Most of the time, you can see debris from a distance, but debris can be blown into the road, forcing cars to move into other lanes and causing accidents. When you encounter debris on the road, slow down and pass it carefully before speeding up again.

Individuals

You may notice individuals pulled over on the side of the road, construction workers, or people crossing the roadway as you drive along the road. Most people will avoid cars' paths, but occasionally you may catch individuals off guard and find them in your route.

Slowdown in residential neighborhoods, school zones, and other high pedestrian areas to prevent hitting people on the road. Make eye contact with pedestrians who cross in front of your car so you know they see you. Drive carefully at night to avoid missing someone in your line of sight.

Something about the lane on the far left has a magnetic pull for some drivers. They not only ignore that the lane is designated for passing/overtaking and that they must quickly move into the travel lane to the right to allow someone else to pass, but they also act unconcerned about the traffic behind them. The rule is simple: the lane on the far left is the overtaking lane, not the fast lane. You are breaching the law and causing traffic danger if you do not overtake and continue driving in that lane.

Stopping Abruptly Without Warning

One of the top causes of accidents on roads and highways is slamming on the brakes in moving traffic for no apparent reason. A hasty decision to cease with little preparation or warning is certain to have consequences. Always be alert of the vehicles behind you, stopping gently and carefully to allow other drivers time to react and adjust.

Forgetting To Use the Indicator Signs

Using the indicator when changing lanes or turning a corner is more than simply good driving etiquette; it's also an essential safety function that alerts other drivers to our intentions. When cars next to or behind us are ignorant of the changes we are making on the road, they are obliged to react to our actions without warning, which is a formula for disaster. Once you've indicated and made your move, remember to turn off the indicator, or you'll be confusing (and annoying) drivers behind you for a long time.

Switching Lanes While Turning

Crossing multiple lanes when turning a corner is a risky and expensive driving error. Some people make such wide bends that they can change lanes at the same time. This can lead to crashes with vehicles in other lanes that are also turning at the same time. The proper procedure is to first perform the turn in your current lane and then indicate that you intend to change lanes.

Riding the Brakes

"Have two feet, must use both" is a rule that should be followed when you're not in your car. Some people, however, believe that keeping the left foot on the brake and the right foot on the accelerator is entirely acceptable. This might result in an unintentional yet dangerous habit of pushing both pedals for a few seconds, generally at a red light, pedestrian crossing, or stop sign. This will not only quickly wear down the brakes, but it may also cause accidents as drivers behind you are compelled to respond to your jerky driving. So, take the left foot out of the equation because the right foot is the right one.

Speeding Through an Amber Light

Some drivers appear to believe that an amber light means 'speed up,' not 'slow down,' and instead press the accelerator rather than the brake. Almost every intersection collision is caused by someone driving through a yellow light or, worse, jumping on a red light. Is it worth sacrificing your life and the lives of others to save those 90 seconds?

Not Stopping at Pedestrian/Zebra Crossings

Motorists in the UAE face a Dh500 fine and six black points if they fail to yield to pedestrians at designated crossings. If there is traffic behind you, turn on your hazard lights to alert them that you have come to a complete stop. And, if you're approaching a major crossroads, expect to have to stop for pedestrians or cars that have stopped for them.

Leaving High Beams On

When driving at night on roads without illumination, high beams are required. These beams, however, have the potential to dazzle oncoming vehicles and distract drivers ahead of you. Use low beams when you see another car's headlights or taillights in the distance.

Improper Adjustments of Rear- And Side-View Mirrors

Side view mirrors that reflect more of the vehicle being driven and less of the cars in front of it restrict the driver from seeing cars directly behind them. This is especially hazardous while changing lanes. To almost totally remove blind spots, both side mirrors should be pointed wide enough to just barely see the side of your car. The inside mirror should be positioned such that you can see the entire back window without moving your head.

Bad Seating Position

While driving comfort is important, being too comfy may not be such a good idea. Sitting too far back behind the wheel or in postures that compromise vehicle control may impede reaction time and reduce visibility. Being overly comfy might also lull a driver into a trance, reducing their awareness of what's going on around them. Stay aware and in control by sitting upright and always having both hands on the steering wheel.

Sitting At a Green Light

Wasting valuable seconds at busy junctions can be highly inconvenient for the drivers behind you, especially those who made a concerted effort to avoid making errors! When you're driving, whether you're moving or stopped, stay in the moment.

Using Your Phone (Even in Hands-Free Mode)

Smartphone integration in many modern vehicles has progressed significantly. Voice recognition and other built-in technologies let you converse and text while complying with hands-free laws. Having both hands on the wheel, however, is no guarantee of safety if you are distracted by your phone call. Your reaction speed may deteriorate if you are more focused on your talk than on your surroundings.

MAINTAINING SAFE FOLLOWING DISTANCES

Keeping a safe following distance is by far one of the simplest yet most frequently disregarded defensive driving regulations. Even if you use every other defensive driving method, you will not be a safe driver until you follow this guideline every time you drive. You will almost always have an escape route or be able to take some form of evasive action if you preserve a reasonable distance from other drivers.

Even at high speeds, if you keep a large enough following distance, your chances of colliding with the vehicle in front of you are quite low.

Determining Your Safe Following Distance

During dry weather conditions, you should leave at least 3 seconds between yourself and the car in front of you. Use a fixed object such as a bridge, tree, or even a crack or shadow in the road to accomplish this. Begin counting when the back bumper of the vehicle in front of you crosses that object... a thousand one, a thousand two, a thousand three, and so on. If you haven't reached 3 by the time your front bumper reaches that same stationary item, you should increase the following distance.

Safe Following Distance in Poor Weather Conditions

When vision is poor, such as in light fog, light rain, or at night, double the following distance to a minimum of 4 seconds.

This will appear to be a significant distance between you and the vehicle in front of you. That's OK. I promise you that it will not make your drive any longer than if you were tailgating.

Adding a few seconds of following distance is a tiny nuisance for a significant benefit should something go wrong. Everyone "thinks" they are following the vehicle in front of them, but rear-end crashes are one of the most regular types of traffic accidents.

You can be much more certain that you're driving at a safe distance if you use the counting strategy for following distances.

Safe Following Distance During Extreme Weather Conditions

When driving in severe weather, such as snow, ice, or heavy rain, you should increase your safe following distance to at least 5 seconds (up to 10 seconds is recommended during intense icing episodes).

This will seem interminable. However, if you are in a rush during severe weather, you pose a serious risk to yourself and everyone around you.

Relax, step back, and maintain your distance. You should not be concerned with the time you get to your destination while driving in hazardous weather. You should be concerned about getting there.

Some people believe that being close to the vehicle in front of them increases their visibility. However, this is exactly how multi-car pileup accidents occur.

Why Following Distances Are Ignored

Many motorists believe that maintaining a close following distance provides them with an edge. Following closely behind another vehicle in heavy traffic allows them to avoid being cut off by other vehicles, allowing them to arrive at their destination faster. However, research shows that it is precisely this type of thinking that leads to rear-end collisions. To make matters worse, what constitutes a safe following distance varies widely from driver to vehicle. A distance that appears completely safe to one motorist may appear excessively near to another.

While many drivers confuse following distance with stopping distance, they are not the same thing. Drivers must be able to perceive potential threats and react to them in order to stop in time. When drivers maintain an appropriate following distance, they have improved visibility, allowing them to see further ahead and anticipate or respond to situations as needed.

When a driver follows another car too closely, it alters his ability to focus. Because the driver hasn't provided himself enough distance and time between the automobile in front of him, he knows he could rear-end it if it comes to an abrupt stop. This fear directs all his attention to that car, as he is concerned that the driver will not suddenly hit his brakes.

When a driver's attention is focused on the vehicle in front of him, he will miss many other things happening on the road around him. According to The Smith5Keys, "aiming high" and viewing "the big picture" are critical to safety, and dangerous following lengths limit the driver's ability to see much beyond the car on which he is concentrating.

Encouraging Safe Following Distances

Fleet safety managers can increase driver safety by educating and reminding them about acceptable following distances. The following distance, unlike other factors such as road conditions, severe weather, or other cars on the road around them, is something that every driver has control over.

Drivers can improve their handling of conditions that contribute to tailgating by receiving instruction. Proper following distance does not imply driving slowly but rather driving smartly.

A driver, for example, cannot drive faster than the vehicle in front of him. The driver might opt to drive at the same speed as before or four seconds later. If the tailgating is caused by the vehicle in front of them traveling too slowly, drivers should be trained to pass the vehicle instead of tailgating them to make a point.

If the professional driver is being tailgated, he should find a means to safely pass the other vehicle. To avoid a multi-car collision, he should increase the gap between his vehicle and the one in front of him.

UNDERSTANDING RIGHT-OF-WAY RULES

Respecting the rights of others on the road is crucial, but the rules can be complicated. General rules, such as halting at a red light or stop sign and yielding to pedestrians, are quite simple. You will, however, come across unusual scenarios at crossroads and while driving on unknown or risky routes. Exercise caution and learn how to manage exceptional circumstances ahead of time to avoid accidents or injury.

The First Vehicle to Arrive Takes the Right of Way

At a four-way stop, the first vehicle to arrive at the junction has the right of way. This regulation always applies when someone has obviously arrived at the stop sign first, regardless of where the vehicle is positioned or in which direction it is traveling. Be aware of aggressive or distracted drivers who may disregard this regulation.

Always Yield to The Right

When two vehicles arrive side by side at a 4-way stop, the vehicle furthest to the right has the right of way. If three vehicles arrive at the same time, the car on the far left should continue to yield until both cars on the far right have passed.

Straight Traffic Takes the Right of Way Overturning Traffic

When approaching a junction head-on with another vehicle, it is critical to employ signals. When two vehicles arrive at a 4-way stop at the same moment, face to face, and one intends to turn while the other intends to proceed straight, the vehicle driving straight has the right of way. Remember that if both cars are traveling straight or turning in the same direction, they can both proceed at the same time because their paths will not cross.

Right Turns Over Left Turns, Take the Right of Way

When two vehicles arrive at a 4-way stop at the same moment, face to face, and one intends to turn right while the other intends to turn left, the vehicle turning right has the right of way. Before entering the intersection, move ahead slowly to signal to other traffic that you are making a turn. The driver going left should wait until the other vehicle has passed completely.

Come To a Complete Halt at A Stop Sign or Red Light

Stop at a stop sign for roughly 2 seconds or until vehicles arrive before you clear the junction. If you're stopped at a red light, keep going until the light turns green. Stop before the white line if there is one in your lane at the intersection.

Wait until all traffic has cleared before crossing the intersection if you have a stop sign, but the street you're crossing does not. Before proceeding, be certain that all vehicles, bicycles, and pedestrians have vacated your path, even if it is your turn to go.

Consider a blinking red light to be a stop sign. A flashing yellow light indicates that you should slow down and proceed with caution.

Stop For Pedestrians

Stop for pedestrians who have begun to cross the street. A pedestrian has the right of way once they begin crossing the street. Stop for pedestrians waiting to cross at crosswalks that are not controlled by a traffic light. In most cases, a pedestrian should not cross a traffic-light-controlled crossing until they see a green signal or a walk sign. If you have a green light and are turning onto the neighboring road, you must still stop for a crossing pedestrian.

Yield To Oncoming Traffic

Suppose you're approaching a major thoroughfare. Wait for approaching traffic to pass before entering the road from a driveway, parking lot, or side-of-the-road parking area. When turning into a main road from a minor road, drivers on the busier road have the right of way.

Treat Bicycles as Motor Vehicles

In all situations where you would yield to a car, yield to bikes. For example, before turning left, wait for an oncoming bicycle to pass.

While bicyclists should be treated as motor vehicles, you should exercise caution when driving around them. Allow bikers as much space as possible, and slow down while passing one.

HANDLING ADVERSE WEATHER CONDITIONS

Bad weather and hazardous driving conditions are all too often. Driving safely in normal winter weather conditions such as rain, wind, snow, ice, sleet, and fog is more critical than ever. Extreme weather conditions, such as hurricanes, tornadoes, heavy rain/snow, and electrical storms, make it even more necessary to practice safety. If an extreme weather system is moving through your area, it is preferable to postpone a vacation and stay at home rather than drive.

Here are some driving guidelines for terrible weather:

Plan

Driving in severe weather is usually more unpleasant and takes longer. If you do not allow enough time to get to your destination and are therefore running late, this will simply increase your stress level and may impair you're driving. Also, before you go, check the weather. If you can avoid the worst of a weather system by taking a different route, do so. You can also think about postponing your vacation till the weather improves. If you decide not to cancel, bring a map with you to avoid getting lost in limited visibility and to show you alternate routes if necessary.

Drive Slowly

This goes along with the last point; in terrible weather, you should drive more slowly than usual. This reduces the likelihood of skids and accidents.

Leave Room in Front

When driving in rain, snow, or sleet, several experts advocate doubling the "cushion" between you and the car in front of you. In these conditions, braking is slower, and you must provide extra space.

Make Sure Your Equipment is in Working Order

In the winter, have your tires and brakes checked more frequently. Check the condition of your windscreen wipers and the cleanliness of your headlights. Dirty headlights can impair visibility greatly, especially in severe weather. Clear the ice or frost from your windscreen and mirrors before departing, and keep them clear with your wipers and wiper fluid throughout the drive. If you need to stop scraping ice or snow, do it in a safe location.

Use Your Low Beams in Fog

Turn on your headlights (low beams, not high beams) if you're driving in fog, whether it's at night or during the day. Your low-beam headlights not only help you see but also other drivers. It is also critical to keep a big following distance and drive slowly in fog, as you may not notice things like another car or a traffic light until it is almost upon you. In fog, stay close to the right side of the road to avoid crossing the center line into oncoming traffic.

Listen To the Radio

During your journey, listen to a radio station that provides road condition information at a low volume. The station may suggest alternate routes or notify you of road closures. Keep it at a low volume so that it does not interfere with your attention; driving in severe weather requires you to be extremely concentrated.

Drive Slowly

This goes along with the last point; in terrible weather, you should drive more slowly than usual. This reduces the likelihood of skids and accidents.

Buckle Up

Wear seatbelts always, both you and your passengers. It is not only the law in most states, but it can also save lives, particularly when driving in inclement weather.

Pull Over if You Need to

If you feel tired, pull over (in a safe place completely off the road) and rest your eyes. Don't be concerned about the time you could "waste" by pulling over; it's a far better risk than being in an accident. Also, if the weather suddenly becomes terrible, it may be a good idea to find a safe area to pull over and wait out the storm. If the bad weather includes deep snow or heavy rain, avoid pulling over into a deep puddle or snowbank.

The Snow and Ice

Driving a car is never "easy," but it is extremely difficult in cold weather. Ask someone with winter driving experience to take you to a vacant parking lot where you may practice driving, turning, and stopping in the snow.

If you must travel, keep your car fully charged to avoid freezing fuel lines. Clear all snow from the car (including the roof), making sure to sweep the taillights and headlights. Keep an eye out for slow-moving vehicles such as snow plows and sand trucks and avoid getting too near — the last thing you need in a snowstorm is a sand-filled windscreen. Avoid passing these cars as well.

Rainy Roads

Roads are filthy environments. A lot of oily and slick substances accumulate on highways as a result of tires churning up gravel and engines spilling oil and other fluids. That is why roads become slick practically soon as it begins to rain. Water pulls those oils to the surface, making them slippery.

If you find yourself in a slick condition and your automobile begins to glide or hydroplane, don't panic or slam on the brakes. Maintain a firm grip on the steering wheel, lift your foot off the accelerator, and let the vehicle coast (without turning the steering wheel) until you feel it regain traction.

Scorching Sun and Fuzzy Fog

Visibility is one of the most important aspects of driving. Visibility can be reduced by both direct sunlight and dense fog. Always keep UV sunglasses in your automobile to combat that annoying fireball in the sky. Consider purchasing polarized sunglasses to minimize glare and increase visibility. The pop-down visor in your car can also assist in reducing glare.

Fog is more difficult to manage than direct sunlight. Visibility can be reduced to less than 14 miles in fog. Keep your speed down since fog might fool you into believing you're driving slower than you are. It's difficult to detect brake lights or traffic signals until you're practically upon them when you can't see far ahead. And just because you can't see doesn't imply that turning on your bright beams will help. High beams, in fact, hinder vision in fog. Use your fog lights if you have them. They will assist you in seeing the road edges close to your vehicle.

CHAPTER 4

ROAD SIGNS AND SIGNALS

T raffic signs play an important role in directing, informing, and managing the behavior of road users in order to make the roads as safe as possible for everyone. This necessitates familiarity with traffic signs. Not only are new drivers and riders required to complete their theory test, but all road users, even seasoned professional drivers, are affected.

UNDERSTANDING TRAFFIC SIGNS, SIGNALS, AND PAVEMENT MARKINGS

Traffic controls are markers, signs, and signal devices that are used to inform, guide, and regulate motor vehicle traffic on the road. These contribute to making driving a safer and more enjoyable experience for all road users. Traffic controllers fulfill one of four functions:

1. Control the speed and flow of traffic on the route.
2. Inform drivers of potential risks or changing circumstances ahead.
3. Inform drivers about local and state road regulations.
4. Help drivers get to their destination by identifying the route or location.

Stop signs, yield signs, crosswalks, traffic lights, and other sorts of traffic control equipment are common. Failure to follow Florida traffic regulations involving traffic control devices can result in a traffic citation with a variety of penalties based on the specific offense. Florida driver's manual covers all traffic signals and signage in the state. Anyone earning their driver's license should read this chapter.

Traffic Signs

Regulatory Signs: Regulatory signs are used to direct traffic by establishing boundaries or issuing orders. These signs are legally binding, and drivers must follow their directions. Stop signs, yield signs, speed restriction signs, and no-entry signs are examples of regulatory signs. When confronted with regulation signs, drivers must take the measures or limits suggested to ensure the safety of all road users.

Warning Signs

Drivers are warned of potential risks or dangerous circumstances ahead by using warning signs. These signs provide drivers with advance warnings, allowing them to change their speed and behavior accordingly. Signs suggesting lane reductions, sudden curves, pedestrian crossings, or wildlife crossings are examples of warning signs. Drivers must take caution while approaching warning signs, slow down, and proceed with heightened awareness.

Informational Signs

Informational signs inform drivers of directions, distances, services, and landmarks. These indicators help drivers navigate their routes and make informed decisions on the road. Highway exit signs, rest area signs, and tourist attraction signage are examples of informational signs. Drivers should pay attention to these signs to ensure they stay on the right path and arrive safely at their destinations.

Colors

The colors used on traffic signs are intended to express specific meanings and assist drivers in comprehending the intended message. Here are the most popular traffic sign colors and their meanings:

Red

Stop, yield, or ban specific acts are indicated by red signs. Stop signs, yield signs, and wrong-way signs are a few examples. To maintain safety, drivers must respect these signs without exception.

Green

Green flags indicate that it is safe to proceed or provide direction and information. Destination signage and parking signs are two examples. Drivers have the option of proceeding or following the instructions provided by green signs.

Yellow

Yellow signs express caution and advise drivers to slow down or be aware of potential hazards. Curve warning signs, pedestrian crossings, and merging vehicles are some examples. When facing yellow signs, drivers should proceed with caution.

Black and White

Black and white signs are frequently used for regulatory purposes, such as speed limit signs or route markers. Drivers must always follow the instructions on black and white signage.

Temporary orange

Temporary orange signs are used for construction or road repair. Drivers should expect to meet construction activity when they notice orange signs and alter their driving accordingly.

Blue signs

Blue signs offer drivers directions and information. Signs denoting rest spots, facilities, and evacuation routes are some examples. During their travel, drivers should pay attention to blue signs for vital information.

Shapes

A traffic sign's shape can often reflect its message. Here are some of the most frequent traffic sign shapes and their meanings:

Octagonal signs are used exclusively for stop signs. Drivers must come to a complete stop when they see an octagonal sign and give the right-of-way as specified.

Upside Down Triangle:

Yield signs are only used with upside-down triangular signage. When approaching an upside-down triangle sign, cars must cede the right-of-way to oncoming traffic.

Diamond-shaped

Diamond-shaped signs warn vehicles of impending risks or perils. Signs for sharp corners, road repairs, and animal crossings are some examples. When approaching diamond-shaped signs, drivers should be cautious.

Pennant

Signs in the shape of a pennant serve as advance warnings of no-passing zones. When they notice a pennant sign, drivers should return to their side of the road and avoid attempting to pass other vehicles.

Round/Circular

Circular signs are only used at railway crossings. Drivers must be prepared to stop approaching trains if they notice a circular sign with railway symbols.

Pentagon-shaped

Pentagon-shaped signs denote school zones or school crossings. In certain places, drivers should use caution and keep an eye out for children and pedestrians.

Horizontal Rectangles:

Horizontal rectangle signage directs and informs drivers. Route markers and guidance signs are two examples. Drivers should pay close attention to the information on horizontal rectangular signs.

Vertical Rectangles

These signs are used for regulatory notices. Stop signs, yield signs, and speed limit signs are a few examples. Drivers must follow the instructions on vertical rectangular signage.

Safe Intersection Navigation

Controlled Intersections

To restrict traffic flow, controlled intersections feature traffic lights, yield signs, or stop signs. When approaching a controlled intersection, cars must adhere to the following guidelines:

Green Light

When driving through an intersection with a persistent green light, drivers should remain alert and look for other vehicles or pedestrians. Drivers should be prepared to stop if the light turns yellow after it has been green for a long time.

Yellow Light

A constant yellow light signifies that the light is changing to red. Drivers should slow down and be ready to safely stop if possible. When the light turns red, it is dangerous to enter the junction.

Red Light

A persistent red light necessitates that automobiles come to a complete stop at the stop line or before entering the intersection. Drivers must wait until the signal turns green before proceeding. If turning right at a red light is permitted, drivers may proceed after coming to a complete stop and checking for any limitations or approaching traffic.

Uncontrolled Intersections

These are intersections that do not have traffic lights or signs to govern traffic. When approaching an uncontrolled crossroads, cars must follow the following guidelines:

Yielding the Right-of-Way

When two vehicles arrive at an uncontrolled intersection from different roads at the same time, the driver on the left must give the right-of-way to the driver on the right. Drivers should continue with caution and, when necessary, yield to other vehicles or pedestrians.

Turning at Intersections:

When turning at an intersection, cars should follow these guidelines:

Right Turns

Drivers should signal their intention to make a right turn at least 100 feet before the turn. They should enter the right lane and approach the turn from the right side of the road. Before making the turn, drivers must yield to pedestrians and oncoming vehicles.

Left Turns

When making a left turn, drivers should signal their intention and move into the far-left lane in the direction they intend to travel. Before making their turn, they should yield to approaching vehicles and pedestrians. Drivers should also be aware of oncoming traffic and double-check that the intersection is clear before proceeding.

U-Turns

Drivers should check for signs forbidding U-turns before making one. Drivers should signal their intentions, move to the right side of the road, and come to a complete stop if permitted. Before making the U-turn, they should yield to approaching vehicles and pedestrians.

INTERPRETING REGULATORY, WARNING, AND GUIDE SIGNS

Traffic signs are essential for guiding drivers and ensuring safe and efficient traffic flow. This chapter will go over the three major types of traffic signs: regulatory signs, warning signs, and guidance signs. Drivers will be able to manage the roads confidently and responsibly if they understand the meanings and relevance of these signs.

Signs of Regulation

Regulatory signs are intended to manage and regulate motorist behavior. They police traffic laws and advise what measures drivers must take. It is critical for drivers to recognize and obey these signs in order to protect the safety of all road users. Here are some examples of common regulatory signs:

Stop Symbols

Stop signs are octagonal and red in color. They compel automobiles to stop completely at an intersection before going. Drivers must cede the right-of-way to other cars and pedestrians when approaching a stop sign.

Yield Indicators

Yield signs are triangular and red and white in color. At a specific intersection or junction, they signal that drivers must cede the right-of-way to other vehicles or pedestrians. Drivers should reduce their speed and be prepared to stop if required.

Speed Limit Indicators

Speed limit signs notify drivers of the top speed permitted on a specific road or segment of the road. These signs are typically circular in shape, with a red circle encircling the speed restriction in black. Drivers must obey established speed restrictions for their own and others' safety.

Signs Prohibiting Entry

No-entry signs are circular in shape, with a red circle and a white horizontal line in the center. These signs advise that entering a specific road or region is forbidden. Drivers are not permitted to enter or travel in the direction indicated by the sign.

Signs of Danger

Drivers are warned by warning signs of potential hazards or risky circumstances on the road ahead. These signs are intended to allow drivers ample time to respond and alter their driving habits. To guarantee their safety, drivers must pay special attention to warning signs. Here are some examples of common warning signs:

Warning Signs of a Curve

Curve warning signs are diamond-shaped and yellow. They denote the presence of a curve or bend in the road ahead. Drivers should slow down and be prepared for changes in road alignment.

Pedestrian Crossing Indicators

Pedestrian crossing signs are yellow and rectangular, with a walking pedestrian image on them. They denote the presence of a specified place where pedestrians may cross the road. At these crossings, drivers must be cautious and ready to yield to pedestrians.

School Zone Markers

School zone signs are typically yellow and rectangular, featuring images of children or a school bus. They alert cars to the existence of a school zone and the need for caution. In school zones, drivers must slow down and obey the reduced speed limits.

Signs of Direction

Drivers can use guide signs to get information about directions, destinations, services, and landmarks. These signs aid drivers in navigating and planning their travels. It is critical for drivers to correctly interpret guiding signs in order to arrive at their destinations without uncertainty. Here are some examples of common types of guidance signs:

Markers for the Route

Route markers are rectangular signs that display the number or name of a certain roadway or route. These indicators help vehicles find the best path to their destination.

Signs of Arrival

Destination signs tell drivers about specific destinations such as cities, villages, or monuments. These signs assist drivers in navigating and making educated judgments on which route to take.

Signs for Services

Service signs alert drivers to nearby facilities and services such as petrol stations, rest stops, and hospitals. These signs help vehicles locate required services along their route.

Exit Signs

Exit signs are essential for highway and motorway vehicles. These signs indicate impending exits and their destinations. They frequently include the names of cities, towns, or specific sites that can be reached via the exit in question. Drivers can plan their trip and effortlessly transition from one road to another by paying attention to exit signs.

Mileage Signs

Mileage signs advise drivers of the distance to certain locations. They assist drivers with estimating the remaining distance to their destination or determining the distance between different exits. Mileage markers are especially important for lengthy trips, allowing drivers to plan rest stops and refueling breaks accordingly.

Motorway Interchange Signs

These signs help vehicles navigate complex motorway interchanges and junctions. These signs warn of impending interchanges and point out which lanes lead to specific exits or directions. Interpreting these signs correctly allows drivers to make timely lane changes and navigate complex highway systems with ease.

Tourist Information Signs

Tourist information signs are intended to give travelers information on nearby attractions, historical sites, scenic roads, or recreational places. These signs are commonly found in tourist destinations, enticing drivers to explore local sites of interest. They provide useful information that can improve a driver's journey and encourage them to visit new areas.

Rest Area Signs

Rest area signs are important for long-distance drivers because they signal the availability of rest spots where they can take a stop, stretch their legs, use toilet facilities, or have a picnic. These signs aid in the prevention of driving tiredness and give a secure area for drivers to recharge before resuming their journey.

REACTING TO TRAFFIC SIGNALS AND ROADWAY INDICATIONS

Reacting to traffic signals and road signs is an essential part of safe and responsible driving. Traffic signals, signs, and roadside markings are intended to manage and guide traffic flow while assuring the safety of all road users. Every motorist must understand the meaning of these signals and indications and know how to respond accordingly.

Traffic Lights

Traffic lights are the most prevalent and easily recognized type of road signaling. They direct the movement of vehicles and people at junctions and contribute to the smooth flow of traffic. The following are the standard traffic signal indications and responses:

Drivers must come to a complete stop behind the appropriate stop line or before entering the intersection when faced with a steady red light. It is critical to stay halted until the light turns green, indicating that it is safe to move.

Yellow Light:

A persistent yellow light signifies that the signal is on the verge of turning red. Drivers must use caution and prepare to stop while approaching a yellow signal. Drivers may proceed through the intersection if it is unsafe to stop, but only if it can be done safely and without endangering other road users.

Green Light:

A constant green light indicates that automobiles may proceed through the intersection if there are no hazards or pedestrians present. Even with a green signal, it is critical to carefully look for approaching vehicles or pedestrians before going.

Arrow Signals:

Arrow signals may be used in addition to the traditional red, yellow, and green lights. These arrows indicate which way to turn or progress through the intersection. Drivers must obey the arrows and yield the right-of-way to other vehicles and pedestrians when needed.

Roadway Markings:

Roadway markings are painted lines and symbols on the pavement that give drivers visual direction. These markers communicate critical information regarding lane usage, parking laws, and other risks. Understanding and responding to road markings is critical for preserving road order and safety. Here are some examples of common road markers and the necessary responses.

Lane Markings:

Lane markings denote the separation of lanes on the road. Drivers should stay within their lane and not cross over solid lane markers unless absolutely required, such as when making a lawful lane change or avoiding an impediment.

Crosswalk Markings:

Markings are used to indicate where pedestrians should cross. To maintain pedestrian safety, drivers must cede the right-of-way to pedestrians within crosswalks and show caution.

Stop Lines:

Stop lines are solid white lines painted across the road before intersections with traffic lights or stop signs. Before proceeding, drivers must come to a complete stop behind the stop line and wait for the appropriate signal or right-of-way.

Yield Lines:

Yield lines are dashed white lines that show where drivers must yield to approaching traffic or pedestrians. When approaching a yield line, drivers must slow down and cede the right-of-way.

Roadway Signs:

Roadway signs are visual markers that notify drivers of crucial information. They provide instructions, cautions, and regulatory guidance. It is critical for drivers to recognize and respond to road signs in a timely and suitable manner. Here are some popular road signs and the appropriate responses.

Stop Signs:

Drivers must come to a complete stop behind the designated stop line or before entering the intersection while approaching a stop sign. Before advancing, drivers should surrender the right-of-way to other vehicles and pedestrians.

Yield Signs:

Drivers must cede the right-of-way to other cars or pedestrians when they see a yield sign. When approaching a yield sign, drivers should slow down and be prepared to stop if required, allowing other road users to progress safely.

Speed Limit Signs:

The maximum permissible speed on a certain route or stretch is indicated by speed restriction signage. Drivers must obey the specified speed limit for their own and others' safety.

Construction Signs:

Construction signs advise drivers about active roadworks or temporary modifications to traffic patterns. Drivers must obey the advice on these signs, such as slowing down, merging lanes, or taking alternate routes.

CHAPTER 5

PREPARING FOR THE DMV WRITTEN TEST

When preparing to take their permit test, many people make the error of not studying enough. They believe the test will be easy or that they already have a basic understanding of their state's traffic rules, laws, and regulations. When they get to the DMV, they realize they were badly incorrect. The permit test can be far more difficult than most people believe. As a result, it's a good idea to do everything you can to receive your permit quickly and pass the test on the first try.

REVIEWING IMPORTANT TRAFFIC LAWS AND REGULATIONS

It is critical that you spend time researching and comprehending the important traffic laws and regulations that govern the roadways as you prepare for the DMV written test. This portion of the chapter will go more into the significance of reviewing these rules and regulations as part of your preparation process. By being acquainted with the regulations of the road, you will not only boost your chances of passing the exam, but you will also lay the groundwork for safe and responsible driving.

Traffic rules and regulations provide a framework for the orderly and safe movement of automobiles, pedestrians, and other road users. They are intended to enhance consistency, reduce the likelihood of accidents, and establish a consistent understanding among all road users. These laws govern different aspects of driving, such as speed limits, right-of-way rules, traffic signs and signals, parking regulations, and laws prohibiting driving while under the influence of alcohol or narcotics.

Consider the following procedures to thoroughly review relevant traffic laws and regulations:

Obtain the Official Driver's Manual

The official driver's manual given by your state's DMV or licensing body is an excellent resource for learning about traffic regulations. It offers detailed information about the rules and regulations applicable to your jurisdiction. Obtain a copy of the manual and read it thoroughly, underlining significant points and taking notes. Keep an eye out for any modifications or changes in the legislation that have occurred since the manual's publication.

Focus on Key Areas:

While it is necessary to have a comprehensive awareness of traffic regulations, concentrate on key areas that are usually assessed on the DMV written test. These may include speed limits, right-of-way restrictions, traffic signs and signals, parking regulations, and legislation pertaining to driving under the influence. Understanding these areas in depth will not only help you pass the test but will also provide you with a solid basis for safe driving.

Use Online Resources:

Supplement your study materials with online resources that include additional explanations, practice quizzes, and interactive activities. Many websites provide practice exams that mirror the format and content of the DMV written test, allowing you to assess your knowledge and highlight areas that need more review. Use these materials to strengthen your learning and acquire confidence in applying the laws.

Take Notes and Create Study Aids:

As you learn traffic laws and regulations, take notes to strengthen your understanding and create study aids such as flashcards or mnemonic devices. Summaries of key concepts, definitions, and important details that you need to remember. These study aids can help your memories crucial material and recall it more efficiently during the test.

Seek Clarification:

If you come across any perplexing or ambiguous portions of the traffic regulations, seek clarification from reputable sources such as driving instructors, internet forums, or official DMV websites. It is critical to understand the laws in order to make informed decisions while driving. Engage in discussions with other learners or experienced drivers to obtain new perspectives and insights.

Practice Application:

Understanding the theory is crucial, but practicing applying the traffic laws in real-world settings is also critical. Analyze how the laws and regulations come into play as you see and experience different traffic situations on the road. Examine how other drivers interact with traffic signs, signals, and right-of-way restrictions. This practical application will strengthen your comprehension and prepare you for real-world driving conditions.

PRACTICING SAMPLE DMV WRITTEN TEST QUESTIONS

Practicing sample test questions is one of the most effective strategies to prepare for the DMV written test. Practicing these questions allows you to assess your understanding of traffic laws and regulations as well as become familiar with the format and content of the actual test. It also improves your exam-taking abilities, making you more confident and prepared on test day.

Familiarity with Test Format

The DMV written test is often made up of multiple-choice questions in which you must choose the proper answer from a list of possibilities. By practicing example test questions, you will become acquainted with the format and build confidence in efficiently navigating through the questions. This familiarity minimizes fear and allows you to concentrate on understanding and accurately answering the questions.

Content Assessment

Sample exam questions span a wide range of traffic laws, regulations, and safe driving practices. Answering these questions allows you to test your grasp of the content and discover areas that need more attention. This self-assessment allows you to judge your readiness and focus your study efforts on key topics where you may need to improve. You can assure a more comprehensive comprehension of the subject matter by recognizing and resolving your weak points.

Test-Taking Skills

Taking practice tests will help you enhance your test-taking abilities, such as time management, reading comprehension, and critical thinking. It teaches you how to approach different sorts of questions, eliminate wrong answers, and choose the most appropriate answer depending on the facts provided. Practicing example test questions sharpens your analytical skills, allowing you to make sound decisions even in new situations. These abilities are essential not only for the written exam but also for safe and responsible driving in real-world conditions.

Here are a few examples:

1. **When you approach a school bus with flashing red lights from either direction, you should:**
   - Continue driving at the same speed
   - Honk your horn
   - Stop until the red lights stop flashing
   - Slow down and pass with caution

2. **If two cars approach an intersection at the same time and there is no signal or signage, who has the right of way?**

   - The car on the right
   - The car on the left
   - The fastest car
   - The biggest car

3. **When driving in foggy conditions, you should use:**

   - High-beam headlights
   - Low-beam headlights
   - Parking lights
   - No lights

4. **A solid yellow line on your side of the road means:**

   - You may pass if the opposite traffic is clear
   - You have the right of way
   - No passing is allowed
   - Reduce your speed and be prepared to stop

5. **When parking uphill with a curb, you should turn your wheels:**

   - To the left, away from the curb
   - To the right, into the curb
   - Parallel to the curb
   - It doesn't matter which way the wheels point

Remember, these are sample questions, and the actual test may include different topics. Be sure to thoroughly study your local DMV's driver handbook to prepare for all possible questions.

(Answers: 1c, 2a, 3b, 4c, 5a)

TIPS FOR PRACTICING SAMPLE DMV WRITTEN TEST QUESTIONS

The written DMV (Department of Motor Vehicles) test stands as one of the first challenges on this road trip. But fear not, fellow road warrior! With consistent practice and strategic study, you can ace this test. Here are some insightful tips for effectively practicing sample DMV written test questions.

The Driver's Handbook: Your Road Map

Just like any epic journey, you'll need a map. In this case, it's the DMV's driver's handbook. This guide is a treasure trove of rules, regulations, and procedures that form the backbone of your test. Read it thoroughly, and strive to understand the 'why' behind each rule, not just the 'what'. As Confucius might have said if he were a driving instructor, "He who understands the rule masters the test."

Online Practice Tests

The internet isn't just for cat videos and food pictures; it's also a fantastic resource for DMV practice tests. These tests mirror the actual exam's format, giving you a virtual taste of the real deal. Remember, practice makes perfect. Or at least practice makes you less likely to confuse a stop sign with a yield sign.

Consistency

When preparing for your DMV test, try to embody the spirit of the steady turtle rather than the cramming hare. Regular, consistent study helps you absorb information more effectively. Plus, it's less stressful than a last-minute study marathon. As the saying goes, "Rome wasn't built in a day," and neither is a knowledgeable driver.

Learning from Mistakes

When practicing, pay attention to not just what you're acing but also what's tripping you up. Every mistake is a learning opportunity in disguise. Understanding why you got a question wrong helps you avoid making the same mistake in the future. As our dear friend Albert Einstein probably would have said if he were teaching Driver's Ed, "Insanity is answering the same DMV practice question wrong over and over and expecting a different result."

Taking Notes

While studying, grab a pen (or a quill, if you're feeling fancy) and jot down the key points. Especially note those areas you find tricky. These notes will act as your secret weapon, allowing for quick revisions and helping you remember crucial details.

Exam Conditions

Transform your practice sessions into dress rehearsals for the real test. Set a timer, find a quiet place, and complete your practice test without distractions. This exercise will help you get used to the pressure of the actual exam day and teach you to manage your time effectively. As the playwright Oscar Wilde might have said if he were a driving student, "Life imitates DMV practice tests far more than DMV practice tests imitate life."

Staying Updated

While the law doesn't change as frequently as fashion trends, updates do happen. Make sure your study materials are up-to-date. Check the DMV website or reliable educational platforms for any recent changes in driving laws or regulations. As they say in the driving world, "Old laws are like old drivers; they occasionally need updating."

TIPS FOR A SUCCESSFUL DMV WRITTEN TEST EXPERIENCE

Taking the DMV written test might be nerve-racking, but with proper preparation and mentality, you can improve your chances of success. We will give you helpful recommendations in this part to assist you in approaching the DMV written test with confidence and maximizing your performance on test day. You may improve your preparation, handle test-day anxiety, and raise your chances of passing the written test by following these guidelines.

Review the Driver's Manual:

The DMV's driver's manual is a wonderful resource that covers all the material you need to know for the written test. Examine the manual completely, paying specific attention to traffic laws, road signs, and safe driving practices. Understanding the material in the driver's manual is critical for correctly answering the exam questions. To emphasize crucial facts and concepts, take notes or use highlighting tools.

Take Practice Tests

Practicing sample DMV written test questions is a great approach to becoming acquainted with the format and content of the actual exam. Use online practice exams or study tools that have realistic test questions. Practice exams not only allow you to examine your knowledge, but they also help you improve your test-taking abilities and boost your confidence. To obtain a thorough comprehension of the content, go over both correct and erroneous responses. Determine your areas for improvement and concentrate your study efforts on those topics.

Understand the Instructions

Before beginning the test, carefully read and comprehend the instructions. Take note of any rules or guidelines that are indicated, such as the time limit for finishing the test, how to navigate through the questions and any additional prerequisites. Understanding the instructions will assist you in navigating the test smoothly and avoiding mistakes. If you have any issues or queries, do not hesitate to seek clarification from DMV personnel.

Time Management

It is critical to manage your time properly during the exam. Understand the number of questions and the time given for the test. Pace yourself correctly, allowing enough time to read and comprehend each question before responding. If you come across a difficult question, don't ponder it for too long. Mark it for future reference and move on to the next question. If you have time after finishing the rest of the test, you can return to the marked questions. Keep an eye on the clock to ensure you complete the test within the time limit.

Read Carefully

To ensure that you understand what is being asked, carefully read each question and response choice. Rushing through the questions can lead to misinterpretation and erroneous answers. Pay close attention to details and keywords that may lead to the correct answer. Reading carefully will assist you in selecting the most appropriate response and minimizing errors. Questions containing negations or double negatives should be approached with caution.

Eliminate Incorrect Options

If you are doubtful about the proper answer, attempt to rule out any obvious wrong answers. Even if you are doubtful, narrowing down your options can boost your chances of selecting the correct answer. Make informed selections based on your knowledge of traffic laws and safe driving practices, and remove options that do not comply with the rules and regulations. Even if you don't know the exact answer, you can sometimes make an educated guess using common sense and reasoning.

Trust Your Preparation

Have faith in your preparation. Remember that you spent time and effort studying and practicing for the exam. Believe in your talents and that you have learned the essential knowledge to appropriately answer the questions. Confidence might assist you in being calm and attentive during the exam. Remind yourself of the time and work you have put into your studies, as well as the progress you have made. Affirmations that are positive can increase your confidence and thinking.

Stay Calm and Manage Anxiety

Test anxiety is common, but it is critical to manage it. Take several deep breaths, have an optimistic attitude, and tell yourself that you are well-prepared. Maintain a steady pace rather than racing through the questions. Take a minute to regroup and concentrate if you are feeling overwhelmed or stressed. To quiet your mind and body, use relaxation techniques such as deep breathing or visualization. Keep in mind that the DMV written test is an opportunity for you to demonstrate your knowledge of traffic regulations and safe driving practices.

Get a Good Night's Sleep and Eat Well

Make sure to obtain adequate sleep the night before the test. A relaxed mind works better, and you will feel more awake and concentrated during the exam. In addition, take a well-balanced meal before the test to provide your brain with the food it needs for peak performance. Avoid foods that are heavy or oily because they can make you feel lethargic or uncomfortable. Maintain your energy levels by staying hydrated throughout the day.

Follow Test-Day Procedures

Arrive at the DMV early on test day to provide enough time for check-in and any necessary papers. Bring all necessary identity documents as well as any additional materials requested by the DMV. Follow any DMV-provided test-day procedures or guidelines. Being organized and prepared will assist in avoiding stress and ensure a smooth testing experience. Before heading for the test, double-check that you have all the relevant documentation and items.

Read Questions Thoroughly

When taking the test, read each question carefully before answering. Don't hurry through the questions because they may contain critical details that will affect your response. Take your time, think about the question, and thoroughly evaluate all your possibilities before deciding. Pay close attention to qualifiers like "always," "never," "most," or "least," as they might have a big impact on the correct answer.

Double-Check Your Answers

If you have time, go over your answers before submitting the test. Double-checking your responses can help you discover any errors or omissions. Pay close attention to any questions you marked for revision, and make sure you give the best answer possible. Use the remaining time wisely to go back and double-check your answers, but don't change anything without a valid reason. Unless you are confident of an error, trust your first instincts.

CHAPTER 6

STRATEGIES FOR SAFER AND SMARTER DRIVING

In this chapter, we will look at key tactics for driving more safely and intelligently. As responsible drivers, we must constantly develop our driving abilities and take initiative-taking measures to protect the safety of ourselves and others on the road. By understanding these tactics, you can lower your chances of an accident, negotiate tricky situations, and make sound decisions behind the wheel. Let us look at the several facets of safer and smarter driving.

MANAGING DISTRACTIONS BEHIND THE WHEEL

Driving necessitates your undivided attention and concentration. However, with the rising use of mobiles, in-car technology, and other distractions, staying focused on the road is getting increasingly difficult.

Put your Phone Away

The usage of mobile phones is one of the most common and harmful distractions on the road nowadays. To avoid this, keep your phone tucked away when driving. Turning off the phone and setting it to "do not disturb" mode can help minimize the temptation to search the internet at a red light or respond to a text message straight away. By putting your phone out of sight and out of mind while driving, you can maintain your focus on the road ahead and reduce the danger of an accident caused by distracted driving.

No Multitask

It is critical to pay whole attention to the task at hand while driving. Anything that occupies your attention or vision while driving might be a distraction. Avoid multitasking while driving, as a rule. Be available at home to eat meals or put on cosmetics, for example, so you can concentrate completely on the road when you are driving. You may improve your awareness and reaction time by removing needless distractions, making you a safer and more attentive driver.

Distraction

Distracted driving puts you and others on the road in danger. It is critical to avoid phoning or texting family members and friends while they are driving, as this can distract them from concentrating on the road. Consider the influence your actions may have on others and encourage safe driving practices in your loved ones. You may help to make everyone is driving environment safer by setting a good example and discouraging distractions.

Talk to Your employer.

It is common for work-related calls and texts to encroach on our personal lives, especially while we are driving, in today's interconnected world. Responding to messages or taking work calls while driving, on the other hand, can be exceedingly dangerous. If you find yourself in this circumstance, talk to your boss about instituting a distracted driving policy. Encourage them to wait until they are safely parked before communicating with personnel. By addressing this issue at work, you can foster a culture of responsible driving and protect the safety of all road users.

Keep Children and Pets Safe

Traveling in a car with children or pets necessitates extra care and measures. Make certain that children are properly strapped in car seats that are appropriate for their age and size. This not only keeps kids safe in the event of an accident, but it also helps to eliminate distractions produced by their movements in the vehicle. Similarly, make certain that your pets are secured in their assigned place in the back of your vehicle, either with pet carriers or safety obstacles. You may reduce distractions and maintain focus on the road by keeping children and pets safe and controlled.

Set a Good Example

Parents have a considerable influence on their kids' behavior, especially how they drive. It is critical for parents to model appropriate behavior for their children by driving attentively. While driving, avoid texting, eating, grooming, or phoning someone. Setting a good example teaches your children responsible driving practices and emphasizes the significance of prioritizing road safety.

Plan Your Journey Ahead of Time

Programming a navigation system or utilizing GPS on a mobile smartphone is a common distraction while driving. Take the time to prepare your itinerary before you start your journey to avoid this. While your vehicle is parked, program your navigation system or ask a passenger to assist you. If you want to use a mobile GPS app, enter your destination before leaving the house. You can retain your focus on the road and minimize any distractions by minimizing the need for navigation adjustments while driving.

Set Rules of the Road

If you have a teen or new driver in your household, consider establishing specific guidelines to assist them in developing safe driving practices. For example, you could limit the number of passengers they can have in the car until they obtain more driving experience. Limiting distractions and potential sources of peer pressure can assist young drivers in focusing on the road and lowering the likelihood of an accident. You provide direction and support for appropriate driving behavior by creating clear norms and expectations.

Avoid Reaching

It is normal to desire to grab anything that may fall into your path while driving. Reaching for objects, on the other hand, can take your focus away from the road and increase the probability of an accident. Refrain from reaching for goods while driving, especially if they have fallen to the floor or are in difficult-to-reach spots. Before recovering the object, choose a safe area to pull over. Always priorities your safety and the safety of others over retrieving personal belongings.

HANDLING ROAD RAGE AND AGGRESSIVE DRIVERS

Dealing with road rage is an important skill that all drivers should have. Road rage events occur on a regular basis, and whether you are the victim or the perpetrator, it is critical to know how to manage such situations calmly and properly. This section will look at successful ways of dealing with road rage and developing safer driving habits.

Driving in a hostile, angry, or aggressive manner is referred to as road rage. Even the nicest people can become furious and aggressive drivers because of it. Road rage can be triggered by minor situations or frustrations on the road, and the consequences can be severe. It is vital to realize that anyone, no matter how calm and cool they are behind the wheel, can become a victim of road rage. As a result, it is critical to arm yourself with tactics for managing your own road rage and protecting yourself from the violent behavior of other drivers.

Managing Your Own Rage on the Road

Rushing and feeling pressured due to time restrictions is one of the key causes of road rage. To avoid this, schedule your trips ahead of time and leave yourself enough time to arrive at your location without feeling rushed. Leaving on time allows you to remain relaxed, lowers frustration, and allows you to drive more quietly.

Listen to *Peaceful* Music

Listening to peaceful and soothing music might assist in distracting your focus away from irritating driving behaviors or acts. Avoid music that may make you feel aggressive or rushed, and instead, choose melodies that promote calm and tranquility. Music can have a significant impact on your mood and help you stay calm and composed while driving.

Consider the Implications

Before succumbing to road rage, take a moment to consider the possible implications of your actions. Aggressive behavior or responding to provocation can result in major consequences such as legal issues, loss of relationships, employment instability, or even physical harm. Remind yourself of the long-term harmful impact road anger may have on your life, and make a conscious decision to prioritize road safety and serenity.

Avoid Aggressive Driving Habits

Driving aggressively, such as flashing lights, blowing horns excessively, tailgating, or indulging in other aggressive driving behaviors, is a clear symptom of road rage. It is critical to recognize your own habits and make a concerted effort to prevent them. Instead, concentrate on defensive driving methods and keeping a safe space between yourself and other vehicles on the road. To lessen the risk of worsening a potentially deadly situation, practice patience and tolerance.

Consider a Passenger Sitting Next to You

Consider having a passenger sit with you to help you control your emotions and actions on the road. This mental exercise helps to instill a sense of accountability and reminds you to drive responsibly. Acting as if there is someone else in the car can help you control your need to be violent or irresponsible.

Take Breaks and Pull Over

When dealing with another driver's road rage, it is critical to prioritize your own safety and well-being. Consider pulling over in a secure spot if you find yourself becoming overwhelmed or agitated. Taking a pause, getting out of the car, and allowing yourself to relax can help to relieve tension and recover your composure. You can resume driving with a clear head after you feel more composed.

Make Your Automobile More Comfortable

The climate inside your automobile can affect your mood and stress levels when driving. Make sure the interior of your vehicle is relaxing and comfortable. Adjust the temperature to your liking, keep the car clean and organized, and keep a cool drink accessible. You may contribute to a calmer driving experience by establishing a nice and comfortable environment.

Defending Yourself Against Other Drivers' Road Rage

Avoid Provocative Behavior:

When confronted with angry or enraged drivers, it is critical not to incite or aggravate the situation. Avoid tailgating other cars, cutting them off, or responding to their angry gestures or statements. Such behavior just feeds aggressiveness and raises the likelihood of an accident or conflict. Instead, concentrate on keeping your own calm and safety.

Drive Defensively:

It is critical to practice defensive driving techniques to protect yourself from other drivers' road rage. Keep an eye out for potential hazards and keep a safe following distance. Avoid collisions by giving aggressive drivers plenty of room on the road. Driving defensively reduces your chances of being involved in a violent interaction.

Ignore Provocative Actions

To keep road rage at bay, avoid engaging in or reacting to provocative actions by other drivers. Avoid making eye contact because it can worsen the situation. Instead, keep your eyes on the road and keep a safe distance from the aggressive driver. Ignoring their behavior reduces the possibility of a confrontation and ensures your personal safety.

Allow Aggressive Drivers to Pass

In some cases, it may be advisable to let aggressive drivers pass and continue their path. This action can help to reduce tension and avoid a dangerous encounter. Remember that your safety is vital, and it is preferable to let an aggressive driver have their way rather than jeopardize your safety.

Maintain Focus on Your Destination

When confronted with road rage events, it is critical to maintain focus on your intended destination. Remind yourself of the reason for your trip and the significance of arriving safely. Avoid becoming distracted by the actions or behavior of aggressive drivers, and keep your focus on the road ahead.

lower Distractions

To lower your risks of inciting road rage in others, reduce distractions in your own vehicle. Avoid using your phone, having extended chats, or listening to loud music that may draw unwanted attention. By remaining focused on the road and minimizing distractions, you reduce your chances of triggering aggressiveness from other drivers.

Install Camera

Installing a dash camera in your vehicle might provide vital evidence in the event of a road rage incident or accident. Dash cameras can record films of aggressive drivers and their actions, which can be used for insurance or legal purposes if necessary. Having video evidence can help you preserve your rights and provide an accurate account of what happened.

DEALING WITH ROAD RAGE AS A VICTIM

If you are the victim of road rage, it is critical that you stay calm and composed. Avoid expressing wrath or aggression, as this may exacerbate the problem. Concentrate on your own safety and avoid confrontations with the aggressive motorist.

Use Your Phone as a Deterrent

If you feel intimidated or dangerous, consider placing your phone close to your ear to give the idea that you are phoning the authorities. This may deter the aggressive driver from engaging in further conflict. If possible, contact the authorities and report the event, providing vital facts such as the vehicle description and number plate number.

Keep Important Information

Try to remember as many details about the situation as you can while being targeted by road rage. Take note of the aggressor's vehicle's make, model, color, and number plate number. Consider making a voice recording or video of the incidents if you have a smartphone. If you need to make a police report or take legal action, this information is critical.

Stay Inside Your Car

To be safe, stay inside your car and lock all doors and windows. Avoid engaging with the angry motorist or exiting your vehicle. By remaining inside, you protect yourself from potential physical injury and establish a protective barrier.

Avoid Driving Home Right Away

If you are being followed or harassed by an aggressive motorist, it is critical that you do not drive directly home. This may reveal the perpetrator your address and put you in danger. Instead, use different routes or travel to a more populated location where other people or law enforcement are present. You can reduce the likelihood of more confrontations or threats by avoiding your home and locating a safer location.

Seek Help and Draw Attention

If you feel intimidated or in immediate danger, take proactive steps to seek help. Make use of your car's horn to draw the attention of other vehicles or pedestrians nearby. To indicate that you require assistance, flash your lights, or engage your danger lights. By attracting attention to the problem, you enhance the likelihood that someone will intervene or alert the authorities.

Document the Incident

If it is safe to do so, photograph or videotape the road rage incident with your smartphone. Take pictures of any visible damage to your vehicle, document the aggressive driver's behavior, and make a list of any witnesses who may be present. When reporting the event to the police or your insurance company, this documentation might be especially useful.

Report the Incident

Once you have safely distanced yourself from the situation, notify the relevant authorities about the road rage incident. Give them all the information you have acquired, including a description of the aggressor's vehicle, the number plate number, and any proof you have gathered. By reporting the occurrence, you help to hold the reckless driver accountable and prevent such incidents in the future.

NAVIGATING FREEWAYS AND HIGHWAYS WITH CONFIDENCE

Navigating motorways and roads can be both exciting and difficult. These roads are built to manage huge volumes of traffic at high speeds, necessitating drivers to be alert and initiative-taking.

Plan Your Route

Take the time to plan your itinerary before you begin your journey. To familiarize yourself with the motorways and highways you will be traveling on, use a reputable navigation system or map. Identify the exits, interchanges, and lane changes you will come across along the trip. A comprehensive grasp of your route can help you stay focused and reduce the likelihood of making last-minute lane changes or decisions, lowering stress, and promoting safer driving.

Merge Smoothly

Merging smoothly with the flow of traffic when joining a motorway or highway is critical for ensuring a safe and efficient driving environment. Use the acceleration lane to keep up with the traffic on the motorway. When it is safe to do so, signal your intentions early, check your blind spots, and merge into the appropriate lane. Stopping or hesitating in the acceleration lane can impede traffic flow and create hazards for yourself and other drivers.

Maintain a Safe Following Distance

Maintaining a reasonable following distance between your vehicle and the car in front of you is an important part of safe driving on motorways and highways. Because of the higher speeds on certain roads, stopping distances must be increased. As a general guideline, leave at least three seconds between yourself and the vehicle ahead. This gap provides you with ample time to react and brake if the car in front of you suddenly slows or stops. Following at a safe distance helps to avoid rear-end incidents and encourages smoother traffic flow.

Use Mirrors and Check Blind Spots

When driving on motorways and highways, it is critical to maintain constant awareness of your surroundings. Check your rearview and side mirrors on a regular basis to be informed of the position and movement of vehicles around you. Always check your blind zones before changing lanes or making any maneuvers by momentarily turning your head to ensure there are no vehicles in those areas. This practice keeps you alert to potential threats and helps you avoid mishaps.

Signal Early and Clearly

Clear communication with other drivers is vital for safe motorway and highway driving. Use your vehicle's indicators to communicate your intentions clearly and early. In advance, indicate any lane changes, imminent exits, or other maneuvers. Early signaling allows other drivers to respond and alter their driving accordingly. To avoid misunderstanding among other drivers, use your signals consistently and cancel them after finishing your maneuver.

Stay in the Right Lane Except to Pass

It is advisable to stay in the right lane on multi-lane motorways unless passing slower vehicles. Typically, the left lanes are used for passing or faster speed. Following this rule contributes to a smoother flow of traffic and lowers the likelihood of collisions involving cars traveling at various speeds. Always be aware of faster-moving vehicles and give them the left lane when it is safe to do so.

Adjust Your Speed to Traffic Conditions:

Traffic conditions on motorways and highways can abruptly change. Maintain vigilance and alter your speed as needed. Reduce your speed to keep a safe distance from the vehicles ahead if traffic is congested or moving slowly. Maintain a close eye on traffic flow and modify your speed to match the conditions. Adapting your speed to traffic conditions promotes safer and more efficient driving.

Anticipate and Plan Lane Changes

Plan your actions ahead of time if you need to change lanes on a motorway or motorway. Use your mirrors to analyze the traffic conditions and locate an appropriate space in the neighboring lane. Check for oncoming traffic and make sure there is adequate room to safely maneuver into the appropriate lane. Avoid making rapid or abrupt lane changes, as this might catch other drivers off guard and lead to an accident. Allow enough time and space to perform your lane shift smoothly.

DEVELOPING GOOD HABITS FOR LONG-DISTANCE DRIVING

Driving long distances may be both fun and difficult. If you're planning a road trip or need to drive a long distance, it's critical to build excellent habits to ensure a safe and comfortable ride.

Get Sufficient Rest Before Your Trip

Make sure you get enough sleep before embarking on a long journey. Fatigue can impact your decision-making skills, reaction time, and general driving abilities. Aim for at least 7-8 hours of sleep the night before your trip to ensure you arrive relaxed and alert.

Plan For Your Route and Rest Stops

Plan your itinerary ahead of time and mark rest stops along the way. Knowing where you may stop to stretch your legs, use the lavatory and have food will help you maintain your energy levels and avoid driver fatigue. Consider scheduling rest breaks every 2-3 hours or as needed, depending on your level of comfort.

Maintain Hydration and Eat Healthy Snacks

Staying attentive and alert while driving requires adequate fluids. Bring plenty of water or other hydrating liquids to sip on during your journey. Pack healthy snacks such as fruits, almonds, and granola bars to keep your energy levels consistent. Heavy or oily meals should be avoided because they can make you feel sluggish and less attentive.

Use Cruise Control Caution

Cruise control is a useful feature for long-distance driving, particularly on motorways and open roads. However, use it with caution and only when conditions allow. Avoid using cruise control in congested areas, on twisting roads, or in bad weather. Remember that cruise control is intended to help you, not to replace your awareness as a driver.

Take Frequent Breaks

Long periods of sitting and driving can cause muscle stiffness and weariness. Take frequent breaks to stretch your legs, stroll around, and recharge your batteries. Take advantage of rest stops to stretch or go for a short walk. This will enhance your blood circulation, minimize muscle tension, and keep you more awake while driving.

Engage in Mental Stimulation

Long drives might become monotonous after a while, raising the risk of tiredness and impaired focus. Keep your mind busy and concentrated by engaging in mental stimulation. Listen to audiobooks, podcasts, or educational stuff of your choice. Engaging in mentally engaging tasks while driving can help reduce boredom and keep your head occupied.

Use Sun Protection and Adjust the Temperature

Long travels frequently include prolonged exposure to the sun's rays, which can be uncomfortable and exhausting. Wear sunscreen, sunglasses, and a hat to protect yourself from direct sunshine. Adjust the temperature inside your vehicle to a comfortable level, making sure it doesn't get too hot or too cold, as this can impair your attention and alertness.

Maintain Good Posture

Maintaining appropriate driving posture is critical for comfort and preventing muscle strain. Adjust your seat posture to ensure optimal spine alignment, and use additional cushions or lumbar supports if necessary. Sit comfortably with your back supported, shoulders relaxed, and hands on the steering wheel. Avoid slouching or adopting uncomfortable poses that can cause discomfort or weariness.

Maintain Focus and Minimize Distractions

Long drives can put your concentration and focus to the test. Keep your attention on the road to reduce distractions inside your vehicle. Avoid using your phone, texting, or indulging in other activities that divert your attention away from the road. Pull over to a safe spot if you need to make a call or address an emergency.

Practice Defensive Driving

Driving defensively is essential for long-distance travel. Anticipate and prepare for probable risks, maintain a safe following distance, and be aware of the actions of other drivers. Drive cautiously in unknown regions and adjust to changing road conditions. Remember that arriving safely at your location is preferable to rushing and taking excessive risks.

CHAPTER 7

OVERCOMING FEAR AND WORRY ON THE ROAD

Fear and worry can have an enormous impact on your driving experience, making it difficult to feel confident and in control on the road. To effectively conquer these feelings, it is critical to first understand where they are coming from. In this chapter, we will look at ways to overcome fear and anxiety when driving.

UNDERSTANDING AND MANAGING DRIVING ANXIETY

Many people suffer from driving anxiety, which can have a substantial influence on their ability to drive safely and confidently. While dealing with driving anxiety can be difficult, recognizing the causes and triggers is the first step towards effectively managing and overcoming it.

Factors Contributing to Driving Anxiety

Driving anxiety can be caused by a variety of underlying circumstances, and it is critical to understand the elements that contribute to your fear. Some of the most common reasons for driving anxiety are:

Past Traumatic Experience:

If you have been in a car accident or had a near-miss occurrence in the past, it can cause a fear response and anxiety while driving. Traumatic experiences can have a long-term impact on your driving confidence and sense of safety.

Fear of Losing Control:

Many people like the feeling of being in control, and the prospect of driving, when external factors can influence safety, can cause anxiety. Driving anxiety can be exacerbated by a fear of losing control of the car or confronting unexpected conditions.

Fear of Judgment:

Some people are anxious because they are afraid of being judged or criticized by other drivers on the road. The worry of making mistakes or being viewed as a "bad" driver can cause anxiety and self-consciousness.

High-Stress Levels:

Existing stress and anxiety in one's life, such as work-related pressures, personal issues, or anxiety disorders in general, might increase driving anxiety. The additional stress can make it harder to concentrate and maintain a cool demeanor while driving.

Lack of Confidence or Experience:

Inadequate driving abilities or a lack of expertise on the road might add to emotions of fear and uncertainty. It can increase your anxiety if you are doubtful of your driving abilities or have limited expertise in particular driving circumstances.

Strategies to Manage Driving Anxiety

While it may take time and practice to overcome driving anxiety, there are various ideas and approaches that can help you manage it efficiently. Consider the following strategies:

Gradual Exposure:

Begin by gradually exposing yourself to stressful driving scenarios. Begin by driving short, familiar routes and progressively increasing the distance or complexity of the driving chores. This steady exposure allows you to gradually gain confidence and lessen nervousness. You can also practice driving in low-stress settings such as vacant parking lots or quiet residential areas before moving on to busier roadways.

Practice Relaxation Techniques:

Deep breathing, gradual muscular relaxation, and mindfulness meditation are among the relaxation techniques that you can learn and practice. These approaches can help you calm your mind and body while driving, minimizing anxiety symptoms. Incorporate these tactics into your everyday routine and use them to improve relaxation before and during driving sessions.

Cognitive Restructuring

Reframe and challenge negative thoughts connected with driving anxiety. Identify and examine any unreasonable or catastrophic driving thinking processes. Replace them with more optimistic and realistic thoughts. Remind yourself of your driving abilities and concentrate on the present moment rather than worrying about worst-case possibilities. You can adjust your mental patterns and build a more cheerful outlook towards driving over time.

Visualize Success:

Visualize yourself driving peacefully and confidently using visualization techniques. Visualize successful trips and outcomes to reinforce good connections with driving and reduce anxiety. Make mental pictures of oneself negotiating difficult driving scenarios with ease. When faced with similar situations in real life, visualizing success can help boost confidence and reduce anxiety.

Practice Defensive Driving:

Take defensive driving courses to improve your driving abilities and knowledge. Defensive driving strategies emphasize anticipating and avoiding potential road hazards, which can boost your confidence and make you feel better equipped to deal with unforeseen events. These courses can provide essential insights and practical skills for safely navigating a variety of driving scenarios.

Create a Supportive Environment:

Surround yourself with sympathetic and understanding people who can offer encouragement and reassurance while you attempt to overcome you are driving phobia. Share your emotions with trusted friends or family members who can offer support and, if necessary, accompany you on practice drives. Their presence might provide additional security and reduce tension.

BUILDING CONFIDENCE AND RESILIENCE

Take a moment and think back to your first time behind the wheel. Feel the unease creeping back? The sweaty palms, the thumping heart, the glazed eyes staring at an ocean of confusing controls? Now, cast your mind to the present day. Look at you now, navigating the asphalt jungle with the grace of a gazelle and the surety of an old sea captain. That, my friends, is the magic of confidence and resilience, two of life's most valuable (and free!) accessories. So, let's delve into how we can build these further, shall we?

Adopting a Positive Mindset

They say life is 10% what happens to us and 90% how we react to it. Start with acknowledging that everyone was once a novice driver. Yes, even that uber-cool guy effortlessly parallel-parking a humongous SUV was once a rookie, anxiously attempting not to curb his mom's station wagon. Making mistakes is a crucial part of learning. Embrace them, learn from them, and watch as your confidence soars.

Skill Up

The more you know, the more confident you'll feel. Take the time to learn about your vehicle, read the owner's manual, and understand what each warning light signifies. Know the rules of the road, the etiquette of driving, and the secret language of blinkers and honks. The more you know about how to handle a situation, the less anxious you'll be when faced with it.

Drive, Drive, and Drive Some More

The ancient Romans had a neat little phrase, "Repetition is the mother of learning." The more you drive, the better you'll become and the more confident you'll feel. Start with short trips in familiar areas, then gradually introduce new challenges, like highway driving, night driving, or city driving. Each successful journey will bolster your confidence.

Buddy Up

There's no shame in asking for help. Having a calm, experienced driver in the passenger seat can be invaluable, especially in the early days. They can provide real-time feedback, reassurance, and even the occasional comic relief. Plus, sharing your driving journey can turn an often-stressful experience into a social one.

Mental Gymnastics

Resilience isn't about avoiding stress but learning how to tackle it head-on. Develop a set of coping strategies that work for you, such as deep breathing exercises, listening to calming music, or practicing mindfulness. Turn each stressful situation into a resilience-building exercise.

Set Your Own Pace

Remember, it's not a race. There's no set timeline to become a "confident" driver. Everyone's journey is unique, so don't compare yourself to others. Set achievable goals, celebrate your progress, and step out of your comfort zone only when you're ready.

COPING WITH CHALLENGING DRIVING SITUATIONS

Ah, the open road! A place of endless possibilities, a symbol of freedom, a witness to countless sing-along sessions, but also, unfortunately, a stage for various challenging situations that test our wit, skills, and patience. Buckle up, folks, as we delve into the practical strategies for coping with demanding driving scenarios. Because, let's face it, not every drive is a tranquil Sunday afternoon jaunt!

Surviving Traffic Jams

There's nothing quite like the joys of being stuck bumper-to-bumper in peak-hour traffic, is there? With horns blaring, engines idling, and drivers weaving lanes like they're competing in grand prix, navigating traffic requires a potent mix of patience, quick reflexes, and strategic driving.

Firstly, patience is your greatest ally. Rome wasn't built in a day, and this traffic isn't going to clear in a minute. Maintain a safe distance from the car in front to prevent any collision in case of sudden stops. Be predictable by signaling your intentions early, and avoid the tempting siren call of "lane-hopping." Often, the illusion of a faster lane is just that—an illusion!

Weather Woes

While driving in a blizzard, hurricane, or downpour isn't quite as fun as belting out your favorite song on a clear sunny day, it's often a necessity. Bad weather can significantly reduce visibility and vehicle control. So, how do you ensure you're not caught out when Mother Nature throws a curveball?

Start by slowing down. It may be a simple tip, but it's often forgotten in the heat (or cold) of the moment. Bad weather conditions reduce tire grip and increase braking distances, so take it easy. Use your vehicle's lights to increase visibility and ensure other road users can see you. Remember, your windshield isn't the only one that's hard to see out of during bad weather; others are in the same boat or car, as it were.

Increase the distance between your vehicle and the one in front to account for longer stopping distances. And remember, your car's technological aids like ABS and traction control are helpers, not superheroes. They can't defy the laws of physics, so don't push it.

Conquering Night Driving

The cloak of darkness brings with it a host of additional challenges for drivers, including reduced visibility, the glare of oncoming headlights, and the increased likelihood of encountering fatigued drivers or wildlife on the road.

To tackle these, ensure your vehicle's lights are in good working condition. Clean your windshield and mirrors to reduce glare and increase visibility. Keep your eyes moving to avoid fatigue, and use the right edge of the road as a guide if oncoming traffic is blinding you. It may sound counterintuitive but try not to look directly at oncoming lights.

Handling Road Rage

Ever encountered a driver who seemed to have swapped their morning coffee for a jug of pure, undiluted rage? It's important to remember that while you can't control others' actions, you can control your own reactions.

Stay calm, avoid making eye contact, and never respond to aggression with aggression. If another driver is dangerously confrontational, consider pulling over (safely) to let them pass or even contacting local authorities if the situation escalates.

TIPS FOR MAINTAINING MENTAL WELL-BEING AS A DRIVER

Driving is more than just operating a vehicle; it's a mental exercise that requires alertness, concentration, and emotional stability. Alas, our minds aren't infallible machines; they're more like temperamental artists, requiring care, attention, and the occasional chocolate chip cookie to function at their best. So, fellow road warriors, here are some tips to keep your mental engine purring smoothly, ensuring you're as fit on the inside as your ride is on the outside.

Pit Stops

On the road to maintaining mental well-being, our first stop is, well, taking regular stops. Just as your vehicle needs to refuel, so does your brain. When embarking on long drives, take a breather every two hours or so. Stretch those legs, get some fresh air, and give your mind a moment to reset. Don't underestimate the rejuvenating power of a roadside snack, a cat nap, or simply taking a moment to appreciate the view.

The Fuel of Champions

Ever heard the phrase, "You are what you eat?" Well, they weren't kidding. The fuel you put into your body affects your mood, concentration, and overall mental well-being. Make sure you're eating a balanced diet rich in brain-friendly nutrients. Opt for complex carbs, lean proteins, and colorful fruits and veggies. And don't forget to hydrate! The human brain is about 75% water, so keep that water bottle handy.

Zen on Wheels

Driving can be stressful, especially in heavy traffic or poor weather conditions. But remember, while you can't control the traffic, you can control your response to it. Practice deep breathing, listen to calming music, or try an audiobook to keep stress levels in check. Don't let road rage get the best of you. Remember, the horn is not a tool to vent your frustration. It's an instrument of safety, not a stress ball!

Tune-Up Time

Just as a well-tuned engine runs better, a well-rested and active body leads to a sharper mind. Make sure you're getting plenty of sleep before hitting the road, as fatigue can seriously impair your driving. Similarly, regular exercise can help reduce stress, improve mood, and increase alertness. Whether it's a morning run, an evening yoga session, or an impromptu dance-off, find what moves you and stick to it.

Minimizing Distractions

In our hyper-connected world, distractions are always a fingertip away. But when you're driving, it's essential to put the phone down and stay focused on the road. Consider switching your phone to 'Do Not Disturb' mode, or better yet, put it out of sight and reach. Let your car be a temporary tech-free haven, a place where you're not a servant to the ping of your notifications. You'll be surprised at how liberating it can feel.

CONCLUSION

As our journey together draws to a close, remember that each page turned, every lesson absorbed, is a new step towards becoming not just a competent driver but a responsible, considerate road user. Throughout this book, *The Driving Bible for Teens*, we've journeyed through understanding traffic laws, learning to control a vehicle, developing a defensive driving mindset, and tackling fears and anxieties associated with driving. Our path, however, does not end here.

Driving, much like life itself, is an ongoing learning experience. Each drive you undertake, whether it's to school, a grocery store, or across the country, is an opportunity to apply and enhance the skills you've learned here. It is my hope that these skills will serve as a sturdy foundation as you continue to build your proficiency, confidence, and enjoyment behind the wheel.

In your hands, you hold more than just the steering wheel. You hold the power to make the roads safer for everyone. I urge you to take this responsibility seriously. Respect the rules, be mindful of others, and never forget the impact of your decisions.

Finally, remember that overcoming fear and worry is a personal journey. Be patient with yourself. Progress may be slow, and that's okay. With every drive, you're growing more comfortable and gaining more experience. Have faith in the process and in your ability to become a confident driver.

Your road to independence, paved with knowledge, experience, and newfound confidence, starts here. May your journey be filled with learning, growth, and endless open roads. Keep learning, keep driving, and keep safe. The world is waiting for you!

Printed in Great Britain
by Amazon